THE ULTIMATE
PROTEIN
POW(D)ER COOKBOOK

THE ULTIMATE
PROTEIN
POW(D)ER COOKBOOK

Think Outside the Shake

ANNA SWARD

THE COUNTRYMAN PRESS · WOODSTOCK · VT

Interior design and composition by Cassie Johnston

Published by The Countryman Press, P.O. Box 748, Woodstock, VT 05091

Distributed by W. W. Norton & Company, Inc., 500 Fifth Avenue, New York, NY 10110

Printed in the United States

The Ultimate Protein Powder Cookbook

ISBN 978-1-58157-253-7

10 9 8 7 6 5 4 3 2 1

To Jon

CONTENTS

THE ULTIMATE
PROTEIN
POW(D)ER COOKBOOK

PREFACE

It was January of 2011 and I was on the phone with my friend Stina.

We were talking about our day-to-day lives and I guess what I was telling her must have sounded pretty boring because when I was finished speaking, all I got was silence. I don't blame her of course—my days weren't exactly the definition of thrill or adventure. Truth is, I was bored. I was on the final year of my PhD and all I did was work on my thesis, read about sociolinguistics and critical theory, submit articles for journals and related publications, and mull over my fieldwork data. I loved the topic I was writing about, don't get me wrong, but I was getting dangerously close to academically imploding. And Stina could tell.

It was at this stage in the conversation that she suggested that I start a blog. At first I said "no way!" and actually laughed at the idea because me? A "blogger"? I just didn't see it. I followed a few blogs, sure, but I never saw myself as authoring one. I thought blogging was something "other" people did, if you know what I mean. Plus, there was the issue that I had no idea what to blog about. Creating an online "diary" didn't appeal to me at all; I was already spending far too much time analyzing data to then want to analyze my own thoughts.

But Stina insisted. She asked me what I love to do. She asked me what was my number one passion. Without hesitation I said that it was food. Food and nutrition, the gym and protein—it was all those things at once.

That's how proteinpow.com was born. It was born out of my desire to share with the world my passion for creative and great-tasting "functional" foods, i.e., foods designed to complement an active lifestyle.

Within a couple of years, the blog had amassed an international readership of hundreds of thousands of people who, like me, were passionate about not only their training and nutrition but also cooking and having fun in the kitchen.

A strong community formed of people who didn't want to give up pizza or pancakes as part of their healthy diet; of people who, like me, liked to chase a good workout with a huge slice of cheesecake; of people who didn't want to buy protein bars full of sugars and fillers but instead wanted to make them at home and make them better—nutritionally superior and a million times tastier.

Before long, our community became global. People from all corners of the world began to follow proteinpow.com and facebook.com/proteinpow, engage with what had by then become a brand, and play with their powders and ingredients—finding new favorites and relishing the fact that a healthy diet doesn't have to be bland and it doesn't have to be boring, not when it can be packed full of fun and flavor instead!

Today, with over 1,500 recipes, **proteinpow.com** represents the largest and most comprehensive resource for protein powder recipes online. Many of my recipes have also been featured in various magazines across the US, Europe, and Australia—including *Oxygen*, *The Grocer*, *Fitnorama*, *Muscle & Fitness*, *Gymgrossisten*, and *Men's Health*. I regularly run protein powder cooking presentations and hands-on cooking workshops with professional athletes and members of a general audience alike. In 2013, the Protein Pow App was launched as a way to share more recipes and continue inspiring people to be creative in the kitchen, try new cooking methods and ingredients, and always, no matter what, think outside the shake!

Welcome to Protein Pow ;-)

Anna Sward

INTRODUCTION
THIS COOKBOOK AND PROTEIN

This cookbook is designed to make healthy eating fun, easy, and above all, enjoyable. It's an offshoot of my website proteinpow.com and it's all about healthy alternatives to the foods you love to cook—and eat! All the recipes found here are packed full of nutrition. They're all sugar-free and devoid of white flour, refined carbohydrates, hydrogenated fats, preservatives, and additives. The vast majority of them are gluten-free too. They're all made with protein powder and contain vegetables, fruits, and healthy fats.

Now, you may be thinking, "there's no way something healthy will taste as good as the real thing." But let me tell you something: these foods often taste better. And they absolutely make you feel better too. No more sugar crashing, carbohydrate overloading, or jumping off the bandwagon of your healthy diet only to feel bad about it afterward. No more bland healthy food and endless plates of vegetable sadness. No more dieting, period! Once you master the art of protein baking, I swear you'll get hooked on it and, if you're anything like me, you'll never crave junk food again.

Why protein you ask? Because we all need protein to function and perform at our very best, whether this is at the gym or in our day-to-day lives. Protein builds and repairs muscles, skin, blood, bones, and cartilage. It's an essential nutrient, needed to support the immune system, balance the hormones, and keep the body functioning. It also makes you feel fuller for longer, controls blood-sugar levels, and ensures a sustained release of energy so you're less likely to want to constantly snack. This, by the way, applies to both men and women. I'm emphasizing this point because, all too often, protein powder is targeted exclusively toward men and is seen as a "man's product", when in reality, women greatly benefit from it too (see pages 4 and 5 for more on women and protein powders).

One thing I'd like you to bear in mind about this cookbook is that it's not written as a medical guide and it's also not a diet book. It is not designed to tell you how much protein you should eat, how you should exercise, or how you should partition your calories and your macronutrients (calculated in kcals, and grams of protein, fat, carbohydrates, and fiber), It is not written to impose a particular dietary protocol upon you. This cookbook is not here to promise you dramatic weight loss, a neatly chiselled six-pack, or extensive muscular gains either. Can it help you in achieving those goals? It absolutely can! But it's not designed exclusively to change your body.

This cookbook is designed to awaken the creative cook in you and make you fall in love with healthy eating by providing you with a number of creative recipes to support your goals, whatever these may be. Maybe you want to snack more healthfully. Maybe you want to compete as a bodybuilder or maybe you want to exploit the full potential of your body by increasing its athletic performance in a particular sport. Maybe you want to lose weight—five, ten, thirty, or even sixty pounds, and you need something to keep you from giving in to your cravings. Maybe you just want to gain a bit of muscle or strength, and/or improve your conditioning at the gym. Maybe you're just bored of chicken or fish with a side of vegetables and rice, and you want some excitement in your culinary life. Maybe you want to make pizza a staple of your diet! If so, this cookbook was written for you.

BUSTING COMMON MYTHS

 Protein powders are only for men who want to build muscle; women shouldn't eat protein powders—doing so will immediately make them bulky.

Proteins—or rather, the amino acids found in protein—are the building blocks of life, and the consumption of them is essential for repairing and building muscle and connective tissue. Protein is also vital for carrying out all our day-to-day activities and feeling and performing our best. This is true whether you're a man or woman.

Whether it's in powder form or not, protein in isolation can't make women "bulk up" or gain muscle. It can't make men automatically "bulk up" and gain a lot of muscle either, not unless they train for it and eat a surplus.

When it comes to women, we simply don't have the testosterone to turn into female bodybuilders overnight. Muscle building is just not that easy; it takes years of focused dedication, strength training, and commitment. So eat your protein powders at will—they won't transform you into the Hulk. No protein powders will, in isolation, give you immense musculature or change your body composition. They won't burn fat or "tone" your body either. Only a solid exercise program, rest, and an appropriately designed diet will do that.

2 If women use protein powders, they should only use "women only" protein powders, i.e., protein powders made for women.

It's hard for me to address this myth without becoming overly impassioned, but let me try: the idea of "women-only" protein powders was conceived by marketers who realized that women often associated protein powders with men and with adding immense amounts of muscle mass. Marketers realized that most women are wary of putting on muscle mass and want to "tone" instead of "bulk." So they figured, "Hey! Let's design a product to cater to women's desire for a lean and 'toned' physique!" And they did: they created women-only protein powders.

To me, these products are a travesty. They're a travesty because they contain the exact same ingredients as the powders sold to men—only they're more expensive and often of a lower quality. Moreover, they frequently include cheaper sources of protein, like soy.

My biggest issue with women-only protein powders, though, is that they sell a myth: the myth that women need special treatment. This isn't true. It's not true when it comes to training (women can and, if you ask me, should train like men) and it's not true when it comes to eating. Sure, women need to eat fewer calories than men to maintain their body composition,

but that's where the biggest difference lies—it doesn't lie in food types. There's no such thing as a "food for men" or a "food for women." That's just someone trying to stamp a myth on a product and charge you more for it.

Reading the label of all protein powders makes a big difference for determining whether the tub you're considering buying should be added to your basket or reshelved. If you read the label, you'll notice the exact same ingredients in powders marketed to women and those marketed to the general population. Sometimes you'll find women-only powders contain some extra ingredients, but often these extra ingredients are useless and not worth the additional cost. Green tea powder, for example, is often added to women-only powders. They add this so they can claim that the protein powder "burns fat." Sure, green tea contains powerful antioxidants that can contribute to the elimination of excess fat (when accompanied by a well-designed diet), but you're better off drinking a few cups of green tea and enjoying the process than you are consuming a bunch of green tea powder in your protein and paying an arm and a leg for it.

3 Protein powders are full of toxic and artificial ingredients.

As I said in the previous section, it's crucial that you always pay attention to a protein powder's ingredient list. This is key to knowing what you're eating and, thus, what you're not. One of the first things I do when I pick up a tub of protein powder is deconstruct its ingredient label. I do this to better understand what each ingredient is, why it's there, and whether I want to eat it. Yes, some protein powders contain artificial ingredients (namely sweeteners and flavorings), but all protein powders shouldn't be assumed to contain them. Also, it's questionable whether artificial sweeteners and ingredients are de facto toxic. I haven't seen any strong data pointing to sucralose, emulsifiers, or any of the gums (i.e., guar gum and xanthan gum) being noxious to human health. Aspartame has been flagged as potentially problematic so I avoid that, but besides that, I haven't seen any data pointing toward the avoidance of another ingredient.

This all being said, I want you to always consider getting one- or two-ingredient protein powders first. You know, unflavored powders with nothing added or just a very small amount of ingredients added to them. When possible, I also urge you to get organic protein powders because, as with all food, sourcing matters and a good-quality protein powder is worth paying a little more for. If you have any questions or need any recommendations, feel free to ask at facebook.com/proteinpow or at the Protein Pow Forum at proteinpow.com/forum.

4 Protein powders are "unnatural," and they're not "real food."

Most protein powders are a byproduct of food manufacturing. As such, of course they're food; there's nothing "unnatural" or "unreal" about them. Take, for example, whey. Whey is derived from cheese manufacturing. Or hemp: hemp protein powder is a byproduct of the production of hemp seed oil. Most egg white protein powders contain just one ingredient: egg whites. There's nothing "unnatural" about these ingredients. They've just been turned into a powder to make their usage more convenient. In any case, like I said above, there are plenty of organic protein powders available in the market today, so if sourcing and quality is an issue, you can get powders that come with a seal of approval and a certificate of origin.

5 Protein powder is "destroyed" when you heat it, because it denatures. Thus, you should never cook with protein powder.

Two things keep people from cooking with their protein powders: unfamiliarity with the process and a misguided fear of "denaturing." All over Internet forums you will find people writing things like, "you shouldn't cook with protein powders because, if you heat them, the protein denatures! And if the protein denatures, it's ruined and you might as well throw the whole thing out."

This is one of the most pervasive myths surrounding protein powders: that cooking them irrevocably damages them because the protein denatures.

Protein doesn't get damaged when you bake or cook it. This goes for protein powders, eggs, meat, etc. Our bodies absorb the exact same amino acids from the protein whether we cook it or not.

Though baking alters the structure of the protein (yes, it does "denature" it), its nutritional value remains unchanged.

Think about this: proteins are basically chains of amino acids that, when heated, can change their conformation (i.e., their structure). When you eat the protein, its molecules are broken down into individual amino acids and are then brought together in your cells, becoming a source of dietary protein. Cooked or uncooked, your body absorbs the protein anyway.

Do we see the protein in our eggs as somehow "damaged" when we cook them? We don't, even though, in reality, the process of heating the egg denatures its protein too, i.e., it changes the naturally occurring amino acid configuration of the egg's protein. But this is a structural change—the essential amino acids in the protein are still delivered, and nutritional content of the egg—or protein powder—remains unaffected.

AN INTRODUCTION TO THE POWDERS

WHEY

Whey protein powder is one of the most popular protein powders in the market today. It is a dairy product, derived from cheese manufacturing, and as a result, it has a slightly milky taste. Its amino acid profile is said to be "complete" in the sense that it contains all essential amino acids (i.e., phenylalanine, valine, threonine, tryptophan, isoleucine, methionine, leucine, lysine, and histidine). Indeed, out of all the protein powders, whey protein has the highest leucine and overall branched-chain amino acid (BCAA) content, meaning that in addition to being high in leucine, it's also high in valine and isoleucine. These BCAAs are key amino acids for muscle protein synthesis, which means they're essential to the maintenance, repair, and growth of muscle tissue. Whey protein powder is rapidly and efficiently absorbed by the body for muscle maintenance

and regeneration—this is why so many people choose to drink a whey protein shake before, during, and after workouts.

Whey protein powder mixes well with other ingredients, it's easy to find in supermarkets and/or health food stores, and it's convenient to drink in protein shakes or smoothies. As you'll find out from reading this book, whey is also great for cooking! But you have to know how. You can't just use whey as a substitute for flour, for example. If you don't know what you're doing, the chances of ending up with something really dry, cardboard-like, and rubbery are pretty high.

One of the first things I hope you learn from reading this book is that, when you're cooking with whey, you must use what I like to call "moisturizing ingredients" or simply "moisturizers." These are things like pumpkin puree, bananas,

cooked sweet potatoes, cottage cheese, cooked beets, Greek yogurt, and/or whole eggs. They're foods that add volume—and bulk—to your batters, helping to offset whey's natural tendency to dry up your foods. Once you learn to integrate these moisturizers into your whey-containing foods, you'll find that you can use whey for all kinds of things besides just protein shakes. You'll be able to use whey to make delicious protein cheesecakes, protein cakes, protein ice cream, protein flan/custards, and glorious oh so glorious protein fluff! A whole world of possibilities will unfold before your eyes.

CASEIN

Like whey, casein protein powder is a derivate of milk and, as such, a dairy based protein powder. It has a similar amino acid profile to whey in that it contains all essential amino acids. But that's where

their commonalities end. While the body digests whey protein very quickly, casein protein powder has a slower digestion and absorption rate. This is why many people who consume casein protein powder do so before bed: to ensure their bodies receive a steady supply of amino acids while they sleep.

In cooking, casein protein powder acts very differently than whey. You'll notice this as soon as you mix casein with water or milk to make a protein pudding or shake: your mixture will be thicker and considerably creamier than it would if you'd added the same quantity of whey. Because of its liquid-absorbing qualities, casein protein powder is great for making protein puddings, protein bars, thick protein fluffs, and protein flans. It's also great to bake with, maybe even more so than whey. That's because, unlike whey, casein has less of a tendency to dry up your baked foods. Instead, it adds a thicker and shall we say "bready-er" texture to them. All that being said, one of my favorite ways of using casein is in protein frostings. It thickens them up beautifully!

PEA

Pea protein powder has an incomplete amino acid profile—it's low in phenylalanine, threonine, tryptophan, methionine, and histidine. It does, however, boast high amounts of five of the nine essential amino acids: lysine, arginine, leucine, isoleucine, and valine. Pea protein powder represents a good protein powder for those wanting to find a vegetarian/vegan alternative to dairy-based protein powders. It is also a wonderful ingredient to cook with, and I often recommend it to people whether they're vegetarian/vegan or not. I recommend cooking with pea protein for two reasons: (1) for its incomplete amino acid profile, and (2) for the way it tastes and bakes.

The first reason may seem counterintuitive—if your goal is creating nutrition-packed meals, why would you want to use an incomplete source of protein? I'll tell you why: because you can complete it. You can enhance the nutritional profile of pea protein powder by mixing it with ingredients that are high in the amino acids that pea protein powder lacks (e.g., eggs or dairy, which are high in phenylalanine, threonine, tryptophan, methionine, and histidine), thereby creating a nutritionally superior food and a more

Pea protein powder is extremely versatile in the kitchen. As you'll see in this book, you can use pea protein powder to make creamy protein sauces, protein soups, protein wraps, savory pancakes, and breads. You can also use it to make protein muffins, protein cupcakes, protein cookies, and (sweet!) protein bars. Much like casein and the other vegetarian/vegan protein powders, pea protein powder absorbs liquids very easily, so because you have to add more moisture to your baked goods, they end up with a wonderful moist consistency. It is for this reason that pea protein powder represents, to me, one of the best flour-replacing powders available on the market today.

"complete" source of protein.

Pea protein is also really tasty! But you wouldn't know this if you went by first impressions. When most people encounter pea protein powder for the first time, they recoil in horror. That's usually because they expect it to smell and taste sweet (like most whey and casein protein powders do) and then are struck by the fact that it doesn't. Pea protein powder smells savory. It tastes savory, kind of like . . . soup! Which isn't, of course, surprising when you consider the fact that it comes from peas.

On its own, pea protein powder doesn't taste as good as whey and casein do, even when it's sweetened with chocolate or vanilla. That's my opinion at least. But guess what? When you couple pea protein powder with other ingredients and use it to cook with, oh! It's like watching a caterpillar transform into a butterfly!

RICE

Those not following a vegan/vegetarian diet frequently overlook brown rice protein powder as a supplementary source of protein. Some cite the fact that brown rice protein has an incomplete amino acid profile, while others simply walk away from the idea—rice protein powder just doesn't capture their attention. But consider the following:

First, though rice protein powder is low in lysine, you can mix it with lysine-containing ingredients (like whey or eggs), to create a more "complete" source of amino acids.

Second, brown rice protein powder bakes beautifully! On its own, its consistency is very

"chalky," so you have to account for this in your mixtures by adding moisturizers. It's also highly absorbent (like the rest of the vegetarian/vegan protein powders) so you have to be careful to not use a lot of rice protein powder in your recipes to prevent them from becoming overly dense.

HEMP

From a nutritional standpoint, hemp protein powder is one of the most "complete" vegetarian/vegan protein powders available. In addition to containing all twenty-one amino acids, hemp protein powder contains several essential fatty acids (EFAs), including linoleic acid, omega-3, and omega-6. It also boasts one of the highest fiber contents of all protein powders. Because of this, however, its carbohydrate content is higher than the rest of the powders.

I'm personally a big fan of hemp protein powder, but the vast majority of people I know aren't. That's because, compared to whey or casein, hemp tastes a bit like . . . grass. It tastes like . . . earth. This, of course, isn't too shocking when you think about where hemp protein powder comes from: defatted hemp seeds.

When you mix hemp protein powder with copious amounts of chocolate, though, you can create delicious protein truffles, cakes, chocolates, and brownies. Cocoa just "masks" much of the "grassiness" inherent in hemp, leaving you with delicious and extremely nutritious chocolatey treats that actually complement the hemp's flavor to perfection!

Like pea, rice, and to a certain extent also casein protein powder, hemp protein absorbs a lot of liquid. That means that, when you use it in the kitchen, you have to use a lot of liquid or moisturizers to ensure you don't end up with a dry mix that looks like you should plant something inside it.

EGG WHITE

If you ask me, I'd say that egg white protein powder is one of the best sources of protein out there. It's easily digested and contains eighteen amino acids in total, including all nine essential ones.

You'll often find egg white protein powder being marketed to those with a dairy-sensitivity or intolerance who may be looking for a dairy-free source of protein. But if you're used to drinking whey or casein protein shakes, don't think you'll find the same thing in egg. I think egg white protein powder tastes horrendous when mixed with just water or milk. It doesn't turn into a creamy shake at all, not unless it contains additional bulking ingredients. It turns strangely gloopy and sticky and . . . hm.

The thing is, though, you always have to think about "reconstituting" it, i.e., mixing it with enough liquids or moisturizing agents to create more of a fresh egg white consistency. When you do this, egg white protein powder provides you with an excellent way to add volume to your baked foods, and in the process, it increases their protein content.

There's one thing I'd like to call your attention to when you're buying egg white protein powder:

When thinking about using egg white protein powder as an ingredient, you have to first think about where exactly you're getting it. There are two types of egg white powder available on the market: the kind you get in the supermarket baking aisle and the kind you get from, say, a sports nutrition brand. The egg white powder you find in the baking aisle of supermarkets is usually sold in small packs and contains only one ingredient: dried egg whites. It's intended for meringues, mousses, and other desserts that require the use of whipped egg whites. Egg white powder sold as a supplement and bought in a tub, however, is a

I love egg white protein powder. You know why? Because I use it as an ingredient. I don't use it as the basis for a protein shake; I cook with the stuff and it's beautiful!

totally different beast. For one, it doesn't whip like the powder does—it never gets any soft (let alone hard) peaks. It also tends to be flavored and contain a few additional ingredients like emulsifiers, which are designed to improve its mixability when mixed into water or milk.

Egg white protein powder is usually a good substitute for whey, and I recommend that if you're intolerant or sensitive to dairy, you use egg in place of whey when making things like protein cakes or cheesecakes.

BEEF

Beef protein powder contains eighteen amino acids, including all nine essential ones. Like egg, beef protein powder is a good substitute for whey protein powder in baking and useful for those who may be, for whatever reason, sensitive to or intolerant of dairy.

You can find beef protein powder unflavored or flavored with chocolate or vanilla. The idea of sweet beef protein powder may sound strange—verging on ghastly—to some of you, I know, but I've tried them all, and guess what. Beef protein powders actually taste pretty good! And they bake really well too, especially in protein cookies, cakes, and cheesecakes. One thing I'd like to say, though, is that beef protein powder tends to be one of the most expensive protein powders out there and is actually not my number one choice for this reason. Also, the idea of powdered beef is just . . . a bit strange to me still. I'd rather eat a big juicy steak, if you know what I mean. But that's just me.

SOY

Last, and in my opinion least, in the world of protein powders is soy protein powder. Soy protein powder is often used by vegetarians/vegans as an alternative to dairy-based protein powders, but I don't personally hold it in high esteem. I don't largely for three reasons: (1) soy protein powder is commonly derived from genetically engineered soy; (2) soy protein powder contains phytoestrogens, which have been argued to disrupt endocrine function by mimicking the physiological effects of estrogen; and (3) soybeans are said to be goitrogenic, meaning they can depress thyroid function.

I also find soy protein powder to be an inferior source of protein, even though if you look at it from an amino acid perspective you'll find that it contains all nine essential amino acids and is relatively well digested by the body. To me, though, the other powders are far superior and less controversial. It is for this reason that you won't find soy-based protein recipes in this cookbook.

PICKING YOUR PROTEIN POWDERS

As you can probably tell by leafing though this cookbook, I use a lot of different kinds of protein powders. Most of them were purchased from supermarkets, health food stores, or online retailers. I never buy protein powders by just reading their front label; I always turn the tubs around and read their list of ingredients first. I urge you to do the same. The ingredients should be the ones doing all the talking, not the name of the powder or what it claims to be able to do ("tone," "burn fat," "build muscle," etc.—this is all just marketing and should be read as such).

When people choose a protein powder for a shake, they usually pay attention to four things: the powder's ingredients, its taste, its mixability (how well it dissolves and mixes with milk or water), and its consistency/texture when added to a liquid (whether it froths nicely, becomes creamy, or gets sticky and lumpy).

When picking a protein powder for cooking, pay attention to the same four things but in a different way. Instead of equally weighing all the above qualities of a protein powder, I'd like you to focus primarily on the ingredients. A powder's taste, mixability, and consistency should come second.

I am of the strong belief that the best protein powders are those featuring the fewest ingredients. You don't want to be using (and eating) a bunch of emulsifiers, fillers, preservatives, and endless ingredients that are there solely to enhance the mixability and consistency/texture of a shake. You'll be using your powders in cooking, so you don't really need any fillers at all—you can add them yourself if a recipe calls for them. By fillers I mean non-protein ingredients like carbohydrates, sugars, vegetable oils, etc. You also don't want to get protein powders with too many thickeners, i.e., ingredients there to give volume to the powder when mixed into a shake. Here I mean things like guar gum and xanthan gum.

Taste, of course, is also very important, and completely subjective. Don't get a whey protein powder you hate or a rice protein powder you find completely unpalatable. If you'd like specific recommendations, don't hesitate to join our forum at proteinpow.com or ask for people's recommendations at facebook.com/proteinpow. Everyone is always willing to help others find a great protein powder! When possible, also buy a small sachet of a powder before committing to an entire tub—this will give you an insight on whether that specific powder is for you.

Finally: sweeteners. Nowadays you'll find protein powders unsweetened or sweetened with aspartame, ace-K (acesulfame potassium), sucralose, stevia, xylitol, or in some cases even erythritol. I could write an entire book on each of these different sweeteners, but for now I only want to say that you should avoid powders with aspartame, reduce your usage of ace-K, go easy on the xylitol and erythritol if they make you bloated, and try to choose stevia whenever possible. That's because stevia tends to be a more "natural" sweetener. That being said, no hard data has been published to prove that sucralose—the most popular sweetener used by protein powder manufacturers—is deleterious to human health. In any case, I say go with the sweetener you like best, and if you don't like any, hey! Just get an unsweetened powder.

ABOUT THE RECIPES FOUND IN THIS COOKBOOK

I want you to approach the recipes found in this cookbook as if you are wearing a wizard's hat, as it were. The point of these recipes is to inspire you to think outside the shake and indulge in foods you may not have previously considered part of a healthy diet.

This is a completely new way of cooking—one that's easy, quick, fun, and all-inclusive. You don't need to know anything about cooking to have fun with the recipes in this book. All you need is to approach your ingredients creatively, listen to your taste buds, and let your inner child run loose.

You will notice right away that this is not your average cookbook. Every recipe features protein powder as well as a number of ingredients that might surprise you. I use sweet potatoes, pumpkin, beans, and beets. I use them to make cakes, pancakes, and cookies! I also use a lot of nuts, seeds, coconut, and spices. I do this because I approach all my recipes with two goals in mind: (1) to create absolutely delicious food, and (2) to ensure they're all highly nutritious and devoid of as many empty calories as humanly possible.

I want you to have fun. My directions are flexible and easy to make your own. Because of this, I stay away from exacting baking times or bakeware specifications. I also don't give you water temperature measurements or bother to separate the ingredients into "dry" and "wet" ingredients. I also include a lot of substitutions in my recipes and invite you to tweak them.

I don't do this to confuse you or leave you in the dark without anywhere to turn, lost and wondering what in the world you're doing. I do this because I want you to be open to experimentation. I want you to pay attention to what's in the oven more than you do the timer. I want you to really get to know your ingredients to the point where you're comfortable playing around with them freely. I'm going to hold your hand, by all means, and walk you through the basics of all my recipes. But after a while, you know what? I want you to run alone. I want you to go crazy with the recipes, to change them, and to play around with your flavors and your ideas.

To help you with this, I'm giving you three quick guides: A protein powder substitution chart, an ingredient substitution chart, and a description of bakeware options.

The protein powder substitution chart is particularly important because I don't want you to feel that, to follow the recipes in this book, you need ALL kinds of protein powders. You don't. As long as you understand what you can substitute for what, you're free to get just one or two kinds of protein and tweak the recipes as you see fit. Do bear in mind, though, that if you do change the types of powder you use, your oven temperatures will differ slightly—that's why I want you to keep an eye on your foods when you're baking and to remove them from the oven as soon as your knife comes out clean.

The ingredient substitution chart is here to guide you in case you want to tweak a recipe to fit what you have in the kitchen or change a recipe's nutritional profile. It's also handy if you want to avoid any particular ingredients. So, say you really want to make the protein brownies made with beets but you passionately hate beets. If that's the case, what you do is simply consult this chart and find a substitution for beets, like cooked sweet potato. Again, you'll have to adapt your baking times whenever you substitute ingredients, and you'll have to keep an eye on your final product more than you do the timer. The point here is for you to play with your food, though, so please substitute freely! And have fun bringing your own foods and flavor combinations to life. :-)

I've also listed basic equipment I use to make the recipes in this book and suggest a number of ways you can use different baking pans to get different types of foods using the same recipes. You don't need to go out there and get every single piece of bakeware I used in this cookbook. You don't need to get silicone muffin cups and giant silicone muffins cups and small, medium, and large silicone cake pans. As long as you get a couple, you're set. Of course, you could get them all if you want more variety, but it's not necessary. The point of this cookbook isn't for you to spend a ton of money on pans, powders, or ingredients. The point of this cookbook is to inspire you to think outside the shake. ;-)

MEASUREMENTS NOTE

I wrote this cookbook using cup and spoon measurements instead of grams, because I find the former far easier to visualize and to follow. You don't need a kitchen scale to make these recipes. All you need is a set of measuring spoons and cups. If you work in grams, though, here are some **approximate** conversions (to be sure, measure out the ingredient in spoons or cups and weigh it):

1/4 cup protein powder = 25 to 31g
2 tablespoons coconut powder = 24g
2 tablespoons ground nuts = 15g
1/4 cup milk (nut, coconut, other) = 60 ml
1/2 cup greek yogurt = 114g
1/2 cup cottage cheese = 113g
1 egg white = 2 tablespoons = 30g
1/2 cup egg whites = 4 egg whites = 120g

STOCKING YOUR KITCHEN

COCONUT MILK: Coconut milk—from a carton—is a fantastic ingredient to add to baked goods instead of regular cow's milk. It's a lot lighter and adds a very nice kind of "nutty" taste to baked foods. It's usually low in calories and most brands have extra calcium added in, so it's a good option for those of you wishing to do away with dairy. I go through coconut milk fairly quickly. My favorite way to use it is in protein pancakes, protein puddings, protein cakes, and protein bars, and coffee/tea.

COCONUT FLOUR: Coconut flour is a wonder food. It is extremely high in fiber, gluten-free, ridiculously low in carbs, and packs a punch when it comes to protein baking. It's very dense, so even though it's pricey, you only need to use very little of it at a time (if you use too much of it, whatever you end up making becomes a bit hard to swallow—literally), so handle this flour with care. I'm a massive fan of its intense "coconuttiness" and like to add coconut flour to my protein bars, pancakes, and pretty much everything I bake.

100 PERCENT COCOA POWDER: I really don't know what to say without breaking into adulation. Cocoa powder is low in fat (compared to, say, a bar of chocolate), low in calories (again, versus solid cocoa), full of antioxidant goodness, and absolutely glorious with each and every protein powder. It goes particularly well with brown rice protein powder, hemp protein powder, and I like to add it to chocolate casein as well—for that extra chocolate BOOM!

ALMONDS: Besides being nutritional powerhouses, plain almonds are extremely versatile. You can make almond milk with them by (1) soaking the almonds overnight in water, (2) throwing the water away the next day, (3) blending the soaked almonds with fresh water plus any flavorings/sweeteners you want (like honey, dates, vanilla, etc.), and (4) straining the mixture to get rid of the solid bits. You can also use almonds to make almond butter by (1) roasting the nuts until they brown and begin to sweat (i.e., to release their fat), (2) throwing them into the mixer, and (3) pulsing them for around 5–10 minutes (the mixture will be grainy at first--that's your almond flour--but then, KAPOW!--it's butter). Of course, you can also eat almonds raw or grind them to make almond flour, which is ground almonds, right before they turn into almond butter.

HULLED OR SHELLED HEMP SEEDS: Sometimes I like to use hulled hemp seeds as a substitute for things like oats or regular flour in protein baking. They're low-carb, high in omegas, nutty, and delicious. You can add them to protein cakes and use them as a thickener for times when you want to lower your carbs without sacrificing texture. You can use them to make, for instance, protein pancakes or gluten-free protein granola. In the granola, hulled hemp seeds are used as a substitute for oats. You can also use them to make protein cookies.

PSYLLIUM HUSK POWDER: Psyllium husk powder is basically just fiber. It's extremely low in carbs and calories. Added to hot water, psyllium husk powder turns into a glutinous mush. If you ever get some stuck on your dish-washing sponge, you'll probably wonder "What in the NAME of . . . is THIS thing on the sponge!?" because it's like . . . some kind of sea creature. Don't ever try to cook it like you would, say, porridge, or use a lot of it in your baking—it'll turn whatever you're making into a strange gelatinous thing. What you should do instead is use psyllium husk powder to make ultra-low-carb crepes, wraps, and tortillas. See page 112.

VANILLA ESSENCE: A must in every baking kitchen. Enough said. I add it to anything and everything in the family of protein cakes, pancakes, cookies, etc. It's especially nice added to things containing cinnamon. Nom, nom, nom. :-D

85 TO 95 PERCENT CHOCOLATE: I'm a big fan of the super dark chocolates. Besides being rich in antioxidants, they're low(er) in sugar, they melt beautifully, and while bitter, add one hell of a punch to protein desserts. If you're a chocoholic and have a tendency to eat entire bars of chocolate at a time, a square of super dark chocolate might be exactly what you need. Why? Because you'll never feel like eating the whole bar. Okay, you might, but it's not as easy as it is to eat a bar of, say, 60 to 70 percent dark chocolate. Really dark chocolate is also fantastic for coating protein bars, because its dark chocolatey-ness complements the bars' sweet fillings beautifully!

OAT FLOUR: Usually gluten-free, high in fiber, low(er) in carbs, and amazing in protein pancakes, cakes, and muffins, oat flour adds that oaty flavor to foods while giving them a thick and rich texture. You can eat it "raw," too, so it's fantastic in protein bars because it makes them softer. It's a great ingredient to have around—and you can make your own. Just grab some oats (gluten-free or regular) and grind them down in a food processor or a coffee grinder until you get a powder. :-)

CINNAMON: The God(dess) of Spices. I could write odes and odes to cinnamon. It's one of my favorite spices on earth. I go through a little jar every two weeks. What to say? Cinnamon is delicious and packed full of nutrition. It's high in manganese and fiber and also rich in calcium. Studies have also shown cinnamon to be great for balancing blood sugar, reducing inflammation, lowering LDL cholesterol and triglycerides, and stimulating immunity.

NUTRITIONAL YEAST: Ever since I got my first jar of nutritional yeast, I've been loving it! It's really tasty added to sauces and pizza, and/or baked into protein bread. It's cheesy, sharp, and nutty, and, combined with extra-virgin olive oil, it's fabulous on chicken.

ORANGE-FLAVORED FISH OIL: Orange-flavored fish oil is one of my favorite things to recommend because it sounds so odd yet is actually really tasty. It tastes purely of orange and not very much of fish (obviously, otherwise I wouldn't be singing its praises). The orange taste is really good added to things like rice pudding or vanilla custard. If you and I were at a store and a bottle of orange-flavored fish oil appeared before us, I would fervently urge to you to get it. It's a magical way to get fish oil into your system and mixes really well into protein oatmeal or vanilla protein pudding.

COCONUT OIL: I'm a big fan of using coconut oil to fry protein pancakes, eggs, and pretty much all the meats and vegetables I eat. Coconut oil has a butteriness to it that fills up your kitchen with an oh-my-GOD-what-is-that-SMELL?! scent. There are many nutritional benefits that have recently been flagged in relation to the consumption of coconut oil. While some are most certainly overinflated, others appear to be well substantiated. All I want to say here is that it is a delicious oil for frying food because it has a higher heating point than other oils.

PEANUT BUTTER: I like to use peanut butter raw when I make protein bars and I like to use it also to bake protein cookies with. Peanut butter is one of the highest-in-protein nut butters, it's rich in healthy fats, and should, I think, form part of everyone's healthy-eating diet.

ALMOND BUTTER: Almond butter is very versatile, and I like to use it in much the same way that I do peanut butter. Both go really well with chocolate, vanilla, and pretty much all stripes and denominations of baked goods. Remember to make it yourself, though, because it's so easy and tasty! Also, when you make it yourself, you can flavor it however you want. You can, for example, add ground cocoa to it for a chocolate spread; you can add vanilla to it, you could add spices, etc.

QUINOA FLAKES: Quinoa flakes are great for gluten-free baking. They're high in fiber, add a bready texture to foods, and act as a good substitute for oats in baking. While I think I tend to use them mostly in savory protein food like breads, quinoa flakes are also good for puddings and cakes. There's just something really nice in their rich and earthy taste. Also, quinoa is one of the highest protein gluten-free grains out there and is also really high in fiber. What's not to love?

PROTEIN POWDER SUBSTITUTIONS

INGREDIENT SUBSTITUTIONS

OAT FLOUR   BUCKWHEAT FLOUR   QUINOA FLOUR   AMARANTH FLOUR

GREEK YOGURT   CREAM CHEESE   COTTAGE CHEESE   QUARK

PUMPKIN (COOKED)   SWEET POTATO (COOKED)   BUTTERNUT SQUASH (COOKED)   BEETROOT (COOKED)

ALMOND BUTTER   PEANUT BUTTER   HAZELNUT BUTTER   SEED BUTTER

BANANA   ZUCCHINI (COOKED)   APPLESAUCE

HONEY   AGAVE   SWEETENER

NOTE ABOUT BAKEWARE: These are the pans I use. All of them, except for the springform, are silicone. I always use silicone bakeware because I find it's best for protein cooking—nothing sticks to your pans and you don't need to grease or oil them. They're also really easy to wash! So I suggest you get at least two of them. Don't be afraid to play around with the recipes found in this cookbook and bake your batters in different pans than I suggest. You'll have to keep at eye on baking times and temperatures, but most of the time it will work. And you'll end up with something new, yours, and exciting.

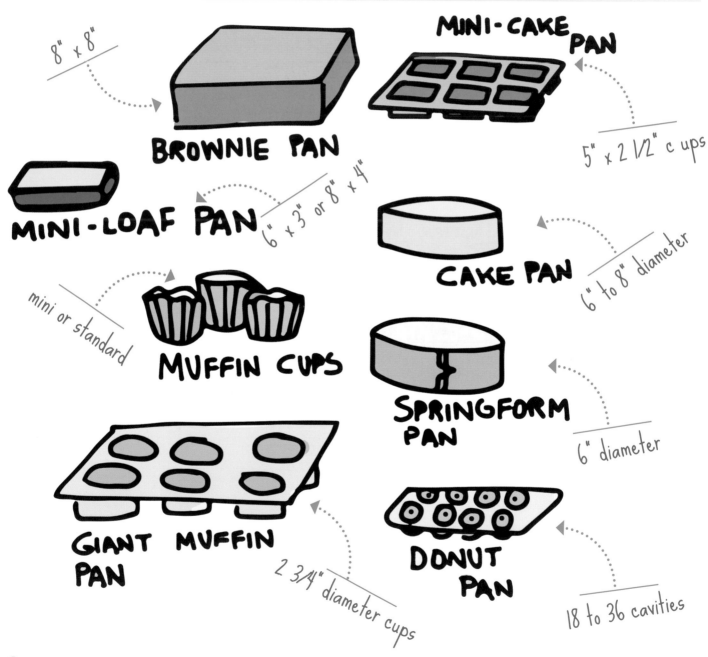

8" x 8"

BROWNIE PAN

MINI-CAKE PAN

5" x 2 1/2" cups

MINI-LOAF PAN

6" x 3" or 8" x 4"

CAKE PAN

6" to 8" diameter

mini or standard

MUFFIN CUPS

SPRINGFORM PAN

6" diameter

GIANT MUFFIN PAN

2 3/4" diameter cups

DONUT PAN

18 to 36 cavities

NOTE ABOUT BLENDING EQUIPMENT: To make all the recipes in this book, I used a handheld or immersion blender with a whisk and a blender attachment. It's perfect for blending batters and for making protein fluff. A good blender can work wonders, and you could also use a standing mixer, hand mixer, or food processor. Their suitability will of course depend on which recipe you're making but, generally speaking, you'll want one item to blend and one to mix; the food processor is for the thickest batters.

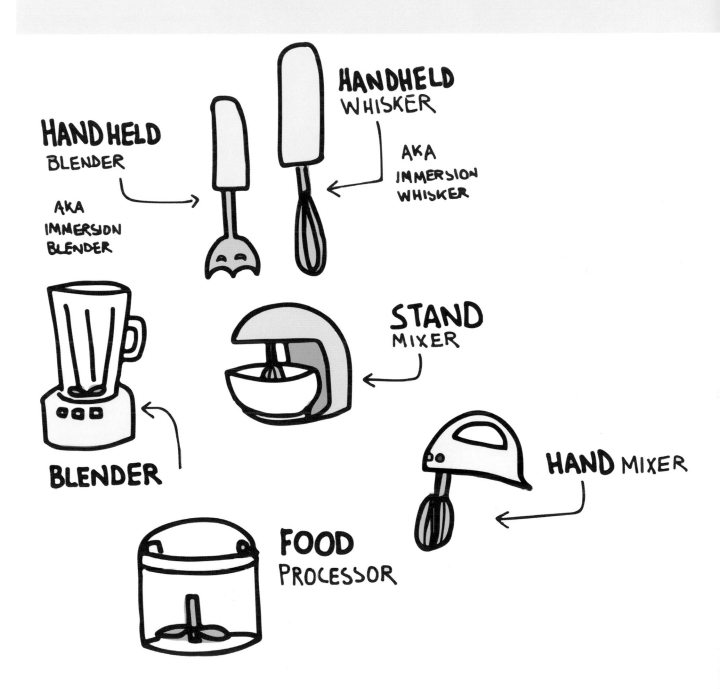

HANDHELD BLENDER
AKA IMMERSION BLENDER

HANDHELD WHISKER
AKA IMMERSION WHISKER

BLENDER

STAND MIXER

HAND MIXER

FOOD PROCESSOR

PROTEIN
PANCAKES
WAFFLES
CEREAL

I CAME UP WITH THIS RECIPE ON A MORNING WHEN I WAS REALLY CRAVING APPLE PIE.

It just kind of came to me—the idea of interlayering slices of steamed apple with cinnamon and vanilla protein pancakes—and I ran with it. The result was delicious! And totally reminiscent of apple pie, which is exactly what I was after. When you make these, remember that you can also add nuts to your pancake mix—chopped pecans or walnuts would be lovely and add an extra texture to the pancakes. You can also top them with a dollop of cream or Greek yogurt! For that full apple pie experience. :-)

APPLE PIE PROTEIN PANCAKES
(FEATURING SIX INGREDIENTS)

SERVINGS

9 medium pancakes

NUTRITIONAL DATA PER SERVING (INCLUDING THE APPLES)

40.7kcals, 4.3g protein, 5.6g carbs, .4g fat, 1.1g fiber

INGREDIENTS

1 small apple

1/2 cup liquid egg whites

1 tablespoon apple fiber (or ground flaxseed)

1/2 medium-size sweet potato, cooked (steamed or baked)

1/4 cup vanilla whey protein powder

1 teaspoon cinnamon

DIRECTIONS

1. Peel and slice your apple thinly. Then, steam the slices over boiling water or in the microwave until they're nice and soft.

2. For the pancakes, blend the egg whites, apple fiber (or flaxseed), cooked sweet potato, and protein powder together. I always blend everything using an immersion blender, but you can also use a food processor or a regular blender.

3. Preheat a nonstick pan that has been further nonsticked with coconut oil, low-calorie cooking spray, or butter.

4. When the pan is hot, start pouring your batter onto it. (When you make pancakes, remember to always spoon the batter onto a hot, hot, hot pan—you want it to sizzle when you pour your pancake mix onto it.) Bring the heat down to medium so the pancakes cook evenly.

5. Once bubbles begin to appear on the pancakes' surface, flip them. Remove to a warm plate and repeat until you've used all the batter.

6. When all your pancakes are done, stack them up with the apple in between, and sprinkle some cinnamon on top. The beauty of using apples this way is that you really don't need any maple syrup on the pancakes. The apple gives them a gorgeous sweetness and, mmmm . . . a wonderful extra flavor dimension.

SUPERNANA BANANA PROTEIN PANCAKES

I named these pancakes "Supernana" not because I wanted to be eccentric and make up a word for the fun of it, no. I named them that because they contain fresh banana as well as banana-flavored protein powder. This meant that they were kind of intense in their bananaess. I'd say that they were "bananalicious" as well, but that sounds ridiculous, doesn't it? So let me just say that they turned out quite tasty and that I think you'll like them too—if, of course, you like bananas. ;-)

SERVINGS
6 medium pancakes
NUTRITIONAL DATA PER SERVING
74k cals, 6.7g protein, 4.7g carbs, 2.75g fat, 1.5g fiber

INGREDIENTS
2 eggs
1/4 cup cottage cheese or quark
(a type of low-fat cream cheese)
1/4 cup banana whey protein powder
1 banana
1 tablespoon coconut flour

DIRECTIONS
1. Blend all ingredients together until you get a smooth batter.

2. Preheat a nonstick pan that has been further nonsticked with coconut oil, low-calorie cooking spray, or butter.

3. When the pan is hot, start pouring your batter onto it. (When you make pancakes, remember to always spoon the batter onto a hot, hot, hot pan—you want it to sizzle when you pour your pancake mix onto it.) Bring the heat down to medium so the pancakes cook evenly.

4. Once bubbles begin to appear on the pancakes' surface, flip them. Remove to a warm plate and repeat until you've used all the batter.

5. Ready to be topped with maple syrup, nut butter, jam or. . . sliced banana?

PEANUT BUTTER & MARSHMALLOW PROTEIN PANCAKES

I often like to chase the weight floor with swimming—laps, thirty to forty minutes, and oh! There's nothing like it. Moving from the grrrrrrrr of the weight floor to the sss-hooosh sss-hoosh ssss-hoosh of the water. It's such a wonderful full-body experience, totally different from squats et al. You just feel. . . so . . . one with your body, your heartbeat, the water; everything else gets silenced completely. But you're not here to read about my love for swimming. You're here for pancakes. So why am I going on and on about swimming? Because swimming's the reason these pancakes happened. Swimming's the reason I woke up ravenous the morning I made these pancakes, and I did what I do when I wake up really hungry: I make protein pancakes. And these? Oh, they were perfect, absolutely perfect—in texture, consistency, flavor, and POW! I couldn't have wished for a better way to start this sunny day—and power up for another swim. ;-)

SERVINGS
6 small pancakes

NUTRITIONAL DATA PER SERVING
61.5kcals, 6.5g protein, 4.1g carbs, 2g fat, 1.4g fiber

INGREDIENTS

1 banana
1/4 cup marshmallow and peanut butter–flavored whey protein powder (or vanilla if you can't find marshmallow and peanut butter whey)
1 tablespoon coconut flour
1/2 cup liquid egg whites
1 tablespoon peanut butter
1/2 teaspoon baking soda

DIRECTIONS

1. Blend all ingredients together and turn the heat under your nonstick pan to high.

2. Add some coconut oil, low-calorie cooking spray, or butter to the pan to ensure your pancakes don't stick.

3. Once your pan is sizzling hot, pour your pancake mix onto it. I like to make small pancakes because they're easier to flip.

4. As soon as your batter hits the (sizzling) pan, turn the heat down to medium, and when you see little bubbles appear on the pancakes' surface, flip them. C'est tout.

BANANA & VANILLA CUSTARD EGG WHITE PROTEIN PANCAKES

Here's a dairy-free protein pancake recipe made with egg white protein powder. I added a banana to the batter because bananas are not only wonderfully tasty alongside all things vanilla and coconut-y, they also lend a robust and hearty body to protein pancakes, making them fluffy, thick, and extra absorbent (an important quality if you're planning to drench them in maple syrup!).

SERVINGS
7 small pancakes
NUTRITIONAL DATA PER SERVING
79.4kcals, 5.1g protein, 9.3g carbs, 1.5g fat, 2.7g fiber

INGREDIENTS

1/4 cup vanilla custard egg white protein powder
1 cup coconut milk
3/4 cup rolled oats (gluten-free or regular)
1/4 cup coconut flour
1 banana

DIRECTIONS

1. Blend all ingredients together until you get a smooth batter.

2. Preheat a nonstick pan that has been further nonsticked with coconut oil, low-calorie cooking spray, or butter.

3. When the pan is hot, start pouring your batter onto it. Bring the heat down to medium so the pancakes cook evenly.

4. Flip when bubbles appear on the pancakes' surface.

5. Done!

THE GREAT BOURBON VANILLA PROTEIN PANCAKES

You'd think it'd get boring, making protein pancakes as often as I do. But it never gets boring—far from it! Because there are endless ways to make protein pancakes and countless ingredients one can use to make them. Take, for example, these pancakes. I made them using pumpkin and ground almonds. Now, most people wouldn't associate these two ingredients with pancakes, but guess what? They're great! I found that out the morning I made these pancakes, and I've been adding pumpkin and almonds to my pancakes ever since.

SERVINGS
8 small pancakes
NUTRITIONAL DATA PER SERVING
85.7kcal, 8.3g protein, 6 g carbs, 3.2 g fat, 1.4g fiber

INGREDIENTS

1 cup liquid egg whites
1/2 cup bourbon vanilla (or regular vanilla) whey protein powder
1/4 cup pumpkin puree
1/4 cup gluten-free oat flour
2 tablespoons ground almonds
1/8 teaspoon sea salt
1 teaspoon coconut oil

DIRECTIONS

1. Blend together everything except the coconut oil.

2. Add the coconut oil to a nonstick pan, and turn the heat to high.

3. When the heat is high enough to sizzle, spoon the batter onto the pan and turn your heat down to medium. You can do as I did and make little ones, or you can make two giant pan-size pancakes—it depends on what makes you nom the hardest.

4. As soon as you see bubbles appearing on the surface of the pancakes, flip them.

5. That's it! You're free to top them with your syrup of choice, nut butter, sliced fruit, or. . .did anyone say bacon?

PEANUT BUTTER & JELLY PROTEIN PANCAKES

SERVINGS

6 medium pancakes

NUTRITIONAL DATA PER SERVING

74.9kcals, 8.9 g protein, 4.4g carbs, 2.3 g fat, .7g fiber

INGREDIENTS

1 egg

2 egg whites

6 tablespoons vanilla protein powder

6 tablespoons rolled oats (gluten-free or regular)

2 tablespoons low-fat cottage cheese

Peanut butter

Jelly (preferably no sugar added)

DIRECTIONS

1. Using an immersion blender, blender, or food processor, blend all the above ingredients until smooth.

2. Preheat a nonstick pan that has been further nonsticked with coconut oil, low-calorie cooking spray, or butter.

3. When the pan is hot, start pouring your batter onto it. (When you make pancakes, remember to always spoon the batter onto a hot, hot, hot pan—you want it to sizzle when you pour your pancake mix onto it). Bring the heat down to medium so the pancakes cook evenly. I made eight mini pancakes here because I wanted to stack them. If you want to make regular-size pancakes, though, go for it.

4. Once bubbles begin to appear on the pancakes' surface, flip them.

5. Layer the finished pancakes with peanut butter and jelly, and . . . boom! Done. :-)

CHESTNUT & STRAWBERRY WHEY PROTEIN PANCAKES

I made these pancakes using chestnut flour. Now, chestnut flour is not a very common flour; it's a bit hard to find in stores, and it tends to be somewhat expensive. But, I tell you, it's worth every penny (or pence, or peso) because it adds such a wonderful depth of flavor to foods, especially pancakes and cakes! It packs a sweet, nutty, and kind of "earthy" punch.

SERVINGS

6 medium pancakes

NUTRITIONAL DATA PER SERVING

56.1kcals, 5.9g protein, 4.3g carbs, 1.2 g fat, 1.3g fiber

INGREDIENTS

1/2 cup liquid egg whites
1/4 cup strawberry whey protein powder
1/2 cup coconut milk (or any milk you like)
1/4 cup chestnut flour
1 tablespoon coconut flour

DIRECTIONS

1. Blend all ingredients together until you get a smooth batter.

2. Preheat a nonstick pan further nonsticked with a bit of coconut oil, low-calorie cooking spray, or butter. Make it hot.

3. Pour batter onto pan and turn heat to medium so the pancakes cook evenly.

4. Flip the pancakes as soon as bubbles start to appear on their surface.

5. Ready to munch. :-)

MAKING A BATTER FOR PROTEIN WAFFLES IS KIND OF LIKE MAKING A BATTER FOR PROTEIN PANCAKES— KIND OF, BUT NOT REALLY.

You see, unlike protein pancakes, protein waffles can't really puff up indefinitely, because they're limited by the dimensions of the waffle iron. So, when you make waffles, your batter can (and should) be a bit more liquid because it'll stay contained in the iron holes, where it'll gain its nice waffle shape as it cooks. That's the theory; now let's move on to some practice! :-)

BANANA PROTEIN WAFFLES

SERVINGS

2 waffles

NUTRITIONAL DATA PER SERVING

96kcals, 3.2g protein, 10.8g carbs, 2.3g fat, 1.8g fiber

INGREDIENTS

1 egg

1/2 large banana

1/4 cup banana whey protein powder

1/4 cup milk

1/4 cup quinoa flour

DIRECTIONS

1. Preheat your waffle iron.

2. Meanwhile, blend together all ingredients until you get a smooth batter.

3. Cook the batter in the waffle iron until . . . well, until the light of the iron indicates they're ready!

BANANA & CHOCOLATE PROTEIN WAFFLES

A few months back, I made two stacks of protein waffles: regular banana ones for me, and banana and chocolate chip for my husband. Mine were very tasty, but his? Whoa, whoa, whoa! Wo-hooooo-hoooa! Total insanity. I tried a bite and, hey . . . Zeus! The man was flipping out. I thought he'd eat the plate. ;-)

SERVINGS

4 waffles

NUTRITIONAL DATA PER SERVING

104kcals, 10g protein, 12.2g carbs, 1.7 g fat, 1.6g fiber

INGREDIENTS

1/2 cup liquid egg whites
1/4 cup vanilla whey protein powder
1/4 cup oat flour
1 large banana
1/4 cup chocolate chips

DIRECTIONS

1. Preheat your waffle iron.

2. Meanwhile, blend together the egg whites, protein powder, oat flour, and banana.

3. Once your batter is nice and smooth, stir in the chocolate chips.

4. Cook the batter in the waffle iron until . . . well, until the light of the iron indicates they're ready.

5. Add syrup, eat them plain, or top with peanut butter.

6. MUNCH!

BLUEBERRY & GOJI BERRY PROTEIN WAFFLES

Here's another tasty way to make protein waffles that integrates berries into the batter and goes deliciously well with maple syrup.

SERVINGS

3 waffles

NUTRITIONAL DATA PER SERVING

145kcals, 15.7g protein, 14.4g carbs, 2.4g fat, 2.1g fiber

INGREDIENTS

1/2 cup liquid egg whites

2 tablespoons goji berries

1/4 cup vanilla whey protein powder

1/4 cup rolled oats (gluten-free or regular)

2 tablespoons cottage cheese (or ricotta or mascarpone)

1 handful blueberries

DIRECTIONS

1. Preheat your waffle iron.

2. Meanwhile, blend the egg whites, goji berries, protein powder, oats, and cottage cheese, until smooth.

3. Carefully stir in the blueberries.

4. Cook the batter in the waffle iron. (You can also use this batter to make pancakes.)

5. DONE!

GINGER & VANILLA PROTEIN FRENCH TOAST

I made this recipe up after a killer squat session at the gym, and oh, oh, oh!

> What better way to chase the squat rack
> Than with a French toast protein POW stack?

(Note: This French toast also happens to bring out the "poet" within.)

SERVINGS

4 slices

NUTRITIONAL DATA PER SERVING

(WILL VARY DEPENDING ON BREAD)

172kcals, 11.6g protein, 21g carbs, 5g fat, 3g fiber

INGREDIENTS

1 cup coconut or almond milk

2 eggs

1/4 cup vanilla whey protein powder

1 teaspoon powdered ginger (optional)

4 slices bread (I used gluten-free whole grain, but you could use any kind)

1 teaspoon coconut oil

DIRECTIONS

1. Whisk together the milk, eggs, protein powder, and ginger. The ginger is optional, but trust me when I say it works incredibly well.

2. Place bread in the egg batter and let it soak for a few minutes.

3. In the meantime, heat up a nonstick pan with a teaspoon of coconut oil.

4. Make sure your pan is sizzling hot, then carefully transfer your bread onto it—you want to make sure that you transport the bread carefully, because the slices will be soggy.

5. When the bread lands in the pan, turn down the heat to medium so the bread cooks through. Then, when ready (after a good 2–3 minutes), flip the bread, let the other side cook, and then . . .

6. BAAAM! Finito! Top it with jam, fruit, maple syrup, honey, nut butter, cinnamon, or some good old bacon, but make sure you're ready—ready to experience French toast–induced bliss! :-D

GLUTEN-FREE PROTEIN GRANOLA

SERVINGS
8 small bowls
NUTRITIONAL DATA PER SERVING
133.5kcals, 12.26g protein, 12.57g carbs, 3.7g fat, 1.6g fiber

This is one of my favorite breakfast "cereal" recipes because it's open to so many variations.

1. To make it even crunchier, add some slivered nuts to the mix along with some seeds. I did this in my first batch, and it was fantastic! (I added sunflower seeds and chopped hazelnuts, mmmm.)

2. For extra antioxidant goodness, consider adding some chocolate chips, carob chips, and/or goji berries to the mix. ;-)

3. If you want your granola sweeter and don't mind the extra carbs, add a tablespoon of honey to the mix. The honey works great because it binds everything together as it bakes and also adds an extra flavor dimension to the whole thing, so, yeah . . . it's good.

4. To lower the carbs, ditch the dates completely— just try your batter before baking to ensure it's sweet enough for you.

INGREDIENTS

2 eggs
1 cup rolled oats (gluten-free or regular)
3 egg whites
3/4 cup vanilla rice protein powder
1 tablespoon coconut oil
6 tablespoons milk (ideally, almond or coconut milk)
1 1/2 teaspoons cinnamon
1 heaping tablespoon chopped dates

DIRECTIONS

1. Preheat oven to 400°F (around 200° C).

2. Stir everything together and spread mixture onto a cookie sheet.

3. Bake for about 20 minutes (check to make sure it's not burning), until nicely browned.

4. When ready, take it out of the oven, and go crazy with it. Break it up with your hands, a fork, a knife . . . hell, you can even use a spork! ;-) Get the pieces as small as you can.

5. To then make it super crunchy, bake it again. Or, if you're not eating it right away, store it like it is, and then, right before eating a bowl, bake it again at a high temperature, so it crunches up nicely.

IMAGINE THIS: YOU'RE A KID AND YOU GO INTO THE FOREST ARMED WITH A HUGE SMILE AND A BUTTERFLY NET.

You start out running, but after a while, you sigh and start frowning because, "Darn, there are no butterflies around!" After an hour of kicking dirt and dragging your butterfly net, wondering why you even bothered with the whole thing, something in the distance catches your eye. Is it a tree stump? A box? What the—NO WAY! It's a MASSIVE treasure chest! You open it and let out a series of screams, because ZEUS! It's GOLD! Lots and lots of GOLD.

When you try to tell your friends about it, you can't even describe your excitement. That's how some recipes make me feel—so ridiculously excited that I don't know how to start. So, I won't. I'll just dive straight into the recipe.

CRUNCHY PROTEIN CEREAL, WAAAAA!

SERVINGS

2 to 3 big bowls

NUTRITIONAL DATA PER SERVING

141kcals, 16.5g protein, 23g carbs, 1.5g fat , 6g fiber

INGREDIENTS

1/4 cup millet flakes

1/4 cup vanilla brown rice protein powder

1 1/2 teaspoons flaxseed powder

3/4 cup liquid egg whites

DIRECTIONS

1. Preheat the broiler (a.k.a. the oven grill).

2. Mix all the above together with a spoon and spread the mixture as thinly as possible onto a cookie sheet.

3. Put it under the broiler for 10–15 minutes, until it begins to smell good and get golden brown.

4. Remove from the broiler, and when it's cool enough, cut it into small pieces. You can do this by hand, as I did, or with a knife (cutting it with a knife will allow you to end up with neater-looking cereal pieces; I did it by hand for more of a cornflakes look).

5. After you do this, stick it back under the broiler for a good 10 minutes, shaking the tray every 5 minutes or so to ensure the cereal browns and crunches up evenly. That's it: AAAAAAA! You end up with these amazingly glorious crunchy bites of flaky cereal! And the beauty is that it STAYS crunchy. I mean, you can keep it in a bag, and it doesn't lose its crunch! In the milk too it takes a while for it to get soggy. Oh, winged mongoose, it's a revolution!

Just like my granola recipe, this one recipe is open to so many possibilities! For example, you can add some nut butter or some actual chopped nuts to the mixture above (if you are into nutty cereals), you can add some grated coconut to it (if you're feeling tropical), you can add raisins (if you're into the abomination that is cereal with raisins), or, well, you can add whatever! Just make this baby yours, and enjoy your cereal with gusto! :-D

THESE ARE A BIT LIKE ANIMAL CRACKERS BUT . . . AIRIER, KIND OF LIKE SWEET TOAST IF THAT MAKES ANY SENSE.

They're really tasty and extremely fun(ny) to eat because you feel like you've reverted to your childhood, and suddenly you can eat an entire zoo! Or, if you treat them as "cereal," you can fish zebras and giraffes out of your milk with a spoon. :-)

ANIMAL PROTEIN CEREAL

SERVINGS
1 big handful

NUTRITIONAL DATA PER SERVING
46kcals, 8g protein, 1g carbs, 1g fat

INGREDIENTS
1 cup vanilla or chocolate whey protein powder

2 cups liquid egg whites

3 tablespoons coconut flour

1/4 cup vanilla pea protein powder

1 tablespoon cinnamon (to swirl on top)

DIRECTIONS

1. Preheat oven to 375˚F (around 190˚C).

2. Blend the above ingredients except cinnamon until you get something resembling pancake batter. Then just pour the batter into a (silicone) brownie pan to bake it as a shallow cake.

3. Bake for about 35–40 minutes or until, when you poke the cake with a knife, your knife comes out clean.

4. Let the cake cool, and, once it's cooled, get out some animal cracker molds. Cut two dozen animals out of the mix and place the animals on a baking tray.

5. Bake the cereal for about 5–10 minutes on each side to ensure both sides brown and "crunch up" nicely. Once everything looks crispy and golden brown, remove the tray from the oven.

6. Eat a bunch and/or store them for later. I recommend storing them in a cereal plastic bag to best retain their crunchiness. If they ever "uncrunch," just stick them back under the grill (or broiler) and boom! Done.

ALLOW ME TO INTRODUCE TODAY'S RECIPE BY WAY OF RHYME:

ICE CREAM PROATS—A "POEM"

In a village by the river
a green monster there lived.
And one morning in September,
a new package he received.

"What is this I have before me?
Looks like ice cream . . . could it be?
Let me rip open this package . . .
It is ice cream! Lucky me!"

So he put it in the freezer,
packed his gym bag, and he went
to the weight floor with a liter
of his 'mino supplement.

He got home after two hours,
hungry as hungry can be.
Didn't have the waiting powers
to even brew a cup of tea
"There is one thing I'll be eating,
and that's homemade protein oats.
A few things just need quick heating,
then I'm ready for my proats."

And it was then that it all hit him:
"Protein ice cream on my oats!
Hot and cold, sweet and sweeter,
oh my Zeus! Holy goats!"

Then he added cocoa powder
to his oatmeal—what a wizard!
With the whey and the ice cream . . .
a protein blast, a nommage blizzard!

THE END

PROTEIN ICE CREAM

"PROATS"

CHOCOLATE PROTEIN OATMEAL & PROTEIN ICE CREAM

SERVINGS
2 bowls

NUTRITIONAL DATA PER SERVING
279kcals, 27g protein, 23g carbs, 9g fat

INGREDIENTS

1 cup milk

1/4 cup rolled oats (gluten-free or regular)

1 tablespoon cocoa powder

1/2 teaspoon toffee stevia (it's optional but really nice)

1/4 cup chocolate whey protein powder

2 scoops protein ice cream (pages 242-243)

DIRECTIONS

1. Mix the milk, oats, cocoa powder, and stevia in a saucepan over medium heat until the oats are cooked and your mix reaches a thick, porridge-like consistency (about 5 minutes).

2. Once cooked, remove the oatmeal from the stove and let it cool for a couple of minutes before mixing in your protein powder. The reason it's best to add the protein powder AFTER the oatmeal is made is because you want to ensure the protein powder doesn't cook, because if it does, it can get all lumpy, and we don't want that—we want our oatmeal smooth and creamy.

3. Get some protein ice cream out of the freezer and put a scoop on top of your oats.

4. Eat it. Eat it as the ice cream melts into your oats and the whole thing . . . just . . . WAAAAA!!!!

PROTEIN
BREAD
BAGELS

A NOTE ABOUT PROTEIN BREADS

Unlike regular breads, protein breads don't rise very much when they're baked. That's why you need to bake them in a narrow enough baking pan (ideally a silicone one) so that the batter has some height before you even bake it. Just play it by ear (or eye, rather) and add enough batter to your pans to almost reach the top.

THE INCREDIBLE ORGANIC WHEY BREAD

This is one of the first whey protein breads I ever made. And the first one I ever loved. I hope you love it too! The softness, the crunchiness of the seeds, and the almost buttery nuttiness of the quinoa and amaranth (which, by the way, is super high in protein, phytosterols, fiber, and lysine!), combined with the subtle sweetness of the whey and the even more subtle sweetness of the fruit . . . pfffffff . . . it's delicious!

SERVINGS
1 loaf
NUTRITIONAL DATA PER 1/10 LOAF
35.4kcals, 2.7g protein, 4.1g carbs, 0.94g fat, 0.7g fiber

INGREDIENTS

1/4 cup unsweetened organic whey protein powder

3/4 cup liquid egg whites

1/4 cup applesauce

1/2 cup quinoa flakes

1/2 cup amaranth flour

2 tablespoons seeds (a mixture of pumpkin seeds, flaxseeds, and sunflower seeds)

1 teaspoon baking powder

1 teaspoon sea salt

DIRECTIONS

1. Preheat oven to 325°F (around 160°C).

2. Using an immersion blender or food processor, blend together all ingredients.

3. Pour into loaf pan—ideally silicone.

4. Bake for 35–45 minutes, or until a knife inserted into the middle comes out clean.

WHEY PROTEIN BREAD WITH GOLDEN FLAXSEEDS

There he is—my dad—slicing a loaf of bread and placing a slice on his plate. He then reaches for a bar of dark chocolate, cuts off a square, and places it on top of the bread. Holding the chocolate in place with his fingers (or sometimes roughly sandwiching the chocolate inside the bread), he dips it into his coffee. The bread gets slightly soggy; the chocolate begins to melt, and then, in one sudden move—BAAAAAAAM! He takes a massive bite and eats the whole thing.

Growing up, this scene was utterly perplexing. I could never understand the appeal of this—bread plus chocolate . . . dipped in coffee? To me that was akin to dipping a cheese sandwich into my hot chocolate.

But now that I am what I consider to be a proper adult, I get it. In fact, I often do it too! With protein bread, of course. It's fantastic because what you get is this somewhat pain-au-chocolat-ish coffee "thing" that's m-mm-mmm—delicious!

INGREDIENTS

1 cup liquid egg whites

1/2 cup organic unflavored whey protein powder

1/2 cup millet flakes

3/4 cup amaranth flour

1/4 cup applesauce

2 tablespoons flaxseeds

1/2 teaspoon baking powder

1 teaspoon sea salt

DIRECTIONS

1. Preheat oven to 325˚F (around 160˚C).

2. Using an immersion blender, blender, or food processor, blend together all ingredients.

3. Pour into loaf pan—ideally silicone.

4. Bake for 35–45 minutes. Do keep an eye on it after 30, though, and take it out as soon as you can stick a knife/fork/chopstick in there and it comes out clean. Allow it to cool, and BOOM! Ready.

SERVINGS

1 loaf

NUTRITIONAL DATA PER 1/10 LOAF

35.4kcals, 2.7g protein, 4.1g carbs, 0.94g fat, 0.7g fiber

I'LL BE HONEST: THIS WHOLE RECIPE WAS AN EXPERIMENT.

I wasn't sure what would greet me when I opened the oven! That's why, when the bread came out looking like it did—like actual bread!—I was like a proud parent. I couldn't stop looking at it, ohhhh-ing and ahhhhh-ing and sweet la la la-ing! And then, well . . . then I cut into it and . . . MAMA MIA! BREAD! Proper "sandwich-able," sliceable, gorgeous-smelling . . . bread!

BROCCOLI BREAD

SERVINGS
1 loaf
NUTRITIONAL DATA PER 1/10 LOAF
50.75kcals, 4.41g protein, 6.1g carbs, 0.8g fat, 1.25g fiber

INGREDIENTS

1/2 cup unflavored whey protein powder

1/2 cup pea protein powder

1/2 cup liquid egg whites

2 eggs

1 large broccoli head, steamed and chopped (around 2 cups)

DIRECTIONS

1. Preheat oven to 350°F (about 175°C).

2. Using an immersion blender, regular blender, or food processor, blend all ingredients together until smooth.

3. Pour into a medium-size loaf pan—ideally a silicone one—and bake for 25–35 minutes, or until a knife inserted into the middle comes out clean.

ORGANIC WHEY PROTEIN PUMPKIN BREAD

I made this protein bread to celebrate the arrival of a new organic whey protein powder that I bought. I made this bread and then used a couple of slices to make a crazy sandwich. Yum!

SERVINGS

1 loaf

NUTRITIONAL DATA PER 1/10 LOAF

54.2kcals, 5.4g protein, 5.9g carbs, 1g fat, 2g fiber

INGREDIENTS

1/2 cup + 2 tablespoons liquid egg whites

1/4 cup pumpkin puree

1/2 cup whey protein powder

1 tablespoon quinoa flakes

1/4 cup buckwheat flakes

1 tablespoon coconut flour

1/2 cup coconut milk

1 teaspoon baking powder

1 teaspoon salt

DIRECTIONS

1. Preheat oven to 325°F (around 160°C).

2. Using an immersion blender, blender, or food processor, blend together all ingredients.

3. Pour the batter into a loaf pan—ideally silicone.

4. Bake for 40–50 minutes, or until a knife inserted into the middle comes out clean.

GLUTEN-FREE FLAXSEED LOW-CARB PROTEIN BREAD LOAVES

There is no reason not to make this bread. It's high in protein, gluten-free, dairy-free, and just good. The spices I use are optional, but I recommend them highly because they lend a sort of festiveness to the bread, a kind of umph umph, mmmmm! if that makes sense. Whichever way you choose to make it, you'll end up with a superb, remarkably moist, fluffy bread that will take care of all your bread needs—and then some!

SERVINGS

1 loaf

NUTRITIONAL DATA PER SERVING

128kcals, 14.5g protein, 5.7g carbs, 4.6g fat, 4.1g fiber

INGREDIENTS

1 cup liquid egg whites

1 cup coconut milk

1/4 cup coconut flour

1/2 cup unflavored pea protein powder

1/4 cup flaxseeds (you can add some chopped
        walnuts to the bread too, and/or some extra seeds)

1/2 teaspoon ground fennel

1/2 teaspoon ground cumin

1/2 teaspoon ground aniseed

Flaxseeds or sesame seeds, for topping

DIRECTIONS

1. Preheat oven to 325°F (around 160°C).

2. Using an immersion blender, blender, or food processor, blend together all ingredients except the flaxseeds or sesame seeds for topping, which you want to keep whole.

3. Pour batter into a loaf pan.

4. Sprinkle flaxseeds or sesame seeds on top to add an extra crunch.

5. Bake for 34–45 minutes, or until a knife inserted into the middle comes out clean.

MULTISEED PROTEIN MINI BAGELS

I'm a big fan of eating mini bagels. I usually eat nine or twelve of them! They look hilarious, and they're really tasty. They're kind of like canapé bagels, or protein hors d'oeuvres. ;-)

SERVINGS

10–18 mini bagels, depending on pan

NUTRITIONAL DATA FOR FULL RECIPE

127kcals, 14.6g protein, 8.9g carbs, 3.9g fat, 1.8g fiber

INGREDIENTS

1/2 cup liquid egg whites

2 tablespoons unflavored pea protein powder

2 tablespoons quinoa flakes

1 1/2 teaspoons amaranth flour

1 tablespoon omega-3 seed mix (a mix of
  pumpkin seeds, sunflower seeds, and
  flaxseeds)

1/2 teaspoon sea salt

DIRECTIONS

1. Preheat oven to 350˚F (around 175˚C).

2. Using an immersion blender, blender, or food processor, blend together all ingredients.

3. Pour into a mini donut baking pan (preferably but remember that, if you're using a bigger baking pan, you would obviously end up with fewer; also, watch your baking time if you decide to make larger bagels!).

4. Bake for 10–12 minutes. Keep an eye on them after 10 minutes and remove them from the oven as soon as they've cooked through.

WHAT'S PROTEIN FLATBREAD?

Protein flatbread is a macro-friendly replacement for regular flatbread. ;-) It's like a wrap but thicker—a lot thicker. It's a cross between protein bread and a protein tortilla. Kind of like pita bread. Protein flatbread is great if you're having a chunky dish that needs scooping, like hummus or baba ghanoush. You can also use protein flatbread to sandwich up some chicken, cheese, avocado, etc.

Another beauty of protein flatbread is that you can make a bunch in advance and keep them in your fridge for three to four days (I keep mine stacked on a plate and covered with plastic wrap). What I like most about protein flatbread, though, is that you can do so many different things with it! You can play around with endless different flavor and texture combinations. For example, you can add chopped nuts, seeds, different herbs and spices, and even veggies! Here are a few variations:

THE FLAVOR POW WAY

Add 1/2 teaspoon sea salt to the mix above along with herbs and/or chopped dried veggies (e.g., paprika, dried parsley, dried rosemary, chopped sundried tomatoes, chopped olives, onion flakes, etc.).

THE TEXTURED WAY

Add hemp seeds, sunflower seeds, pumpkin seeds, or chia seeds to the mix. Consider also adding chopped nuts to the mix before frying! Chopped walnuts and chopped pistachios are especially delicious. You could also throw in a tablespoon or two of coconut flakes. :-)

THE LOWER-CARB WAY

Use 2 tablespoons of rolled oats (gluten-free or regular) instead of 1/4 cup, and add 2 tablespoons flaxseeds to the mix. If you want them lower still in carbs, replace the oats completely by using all flaxseeds or a combo of coconut flour and ground almonds. Just make sure you add an extra 2 tablespoons egg white to the batter if you do that. :-)

PROTEIN FLATBREAD

SERVINGS
2 flatbreads

NUTRITIONAL DATA PER SERVING
164.5kcals, 22.5g protein, 11g carbs, 1.5g fat

INGREDIENTS

1/4 cup rolled oats (gluten-free or regular)
1/4 cup unflavored pea protein powder
1/4 cup liquid egg whites
1 1/2 teaspoons coconut flour (this is
    optional but adds a chunkier texture, so it's
    nice if you like that)
1/2 cup almond milk or coconut milk

DIRECTIONS

1. Using a fork or spoon, mix all ingredients together in a bowl.

2. Preheat a nonstick pan, further nonsticked with a bit of coconut oil or low-calorie cooking spray.

3. Wait until the pan gets hot, hot, hot, and then pour half the mix in, spreading it around with a spatula to ensure it covers the base of the pan.

4. As soon as the batter lands in the pan, turn the heat down to medium-low and wait until the bottom of the flatbread has cooked. Once it has: boom—flip it and remove it from the pan.

5. Let the flatbread cool before eating. I actually like to leave mine in the fridge for at least 2 hours so they firm up and become a bit more like a tortilla.

GLUTEN-FREE PUMPKIN-SEED PROTEIN OATCAKES

Welcome to a recipe for protein oatcakes! These are hearty crackers that work with both sweet and savory toppings. I strongly recommend you give them a shot. You can make the oatcakes sweet by using, for example, vanilla whey protein powder! This will transform them into a more cookie-type cracker. Or you can just make them plain and top them with things like cheese, serrano ham, nut butter, roast beef, cottage cheese, and did someone say caviar?

SERVINGS

4 oatcakes

NUTRITIONAL DATA PER SERVING

127kcals, 7.5g protein, 13.8g carbs, 4.2g fat, 2.3g fiber

INGREDIENTS

1/2 cup rolled oats (gluten-free or regular)

1 egg

2 tablespoons unflavored whey protein powder

2 tablespoons pumpkin seeds

DIRECTIONS

1. Preheat oven to 350°F (around 175°C) and line a cookie sheet with parchment paper, or use a nonstick cookie sheet.

2. Using an immersion blender, blender, or food processor, blend together all ingredients. You'll notice that the mix is really sticky; that's okay.

3. Spread it on the cookie sheet thinly, as if you were making one giant flat cookie.

4. Bake for about 15 minutes, or until it's firm to the touch.

5. Remove from the oven and when cool, use your circular protein powder scoop, cookie cutter, or an upside-down glass to cut out some circles.

6. You'll get four to five circles out of the mix above, depending on which size scoop you use to cut them. You can then just eat them like they are, OR you can grill them further so they get extra crunchy. And, that's it! Done. :-D

THE ULTIMATE PROTEIN SCONE RECIPE

Did you know that scones is pronounced "scoh-ns"? I didn't until very recently, when I went to a café and was proven wrong by the waiter. For years I've been saying "scow-ns"!

Oh well, that's neither here nor there. Let's talk about this recipe. I want you to play around with it—to add some herbs and/or spices to the mix. You can turn them into rosemary and thyme scones or sundried tomato scones. You can add some raisins and cinnamon and turn them into cinnamon scones. You can even add some pecans and walnuts to the batter! Just have fun and follow your taste buds, because this is an incredibly simple and yummy recipe. You have nothing to lose and oh so much m-mm-mmm! to gain. ;-)

SERVINGS
6 scones
NUTRITIONAL DATA PER SERVING
111.5kcals, 11.8g protein, 8.9g carbs, 2g fat, 3.2g fiber

INGREDIENTS
1 cup liquid egg whites
1/2 cup unflavored pea protein powder, rice protein powder, or another unflavored veggie protein powder blend
1 cup rolled oats (gluten-free or regular)
1/4 cup coconut flour
1/2 teaspoon baking powder
1/2 teaspoon sea salt

DIRECTIONS
1. Preheat oven to 350°F (around 175°C) and line a cookie sheet with parchment paper, or use a nonstick cookie sheet.

2. Using an immersion blender, blender, or food processor, blend together all ingredients.

3. Spoon six scone shapes onto the cookie sheet.

4. Bake for 25–30 minutes, or until fully cooked.

BLUEBERRY & RASPBERRY PROTEIN BREAD

A loaf of protein bread: It's easy to make and quick to bake, no need for a shake or a big breakfast steak. You can cut yourself a slice (or seven!), and top freely with butter (it's heaven!) and . . . enough of my "rhyming." Here's the recipe for this, a delish loaf of protein pow to start your day with or enjoy post-workout. It goes fantastically well topped with organic grass-fed butter, nut butter, avocado, or of course, solo, next to a cup of coffee or some tea. If you're into kicking the whole thing up a notch, you could even grab several slices of this bread, coat them in egg, and pan-fry them for a plate of insanely good protein French toast!

SERVINGS

1 loaf

NUTRITIONAL DATA PER 1/8 LOAF

75.7kcals, 9.4g protein, 4.6g carbs, 1g fat, 2g fiber

INGREDIENTS

1/2 cup rolled oats (gluten-free or regular)

1/2 cup vanilla brown rice protein powder

1 cup liquid egg whites

3 tablespoons coconut flour

1/2 teaspoon baking soda

1 cup fresh or frozen raspberries and blueberries

DIRECTIONS

1. Preheat oven to 350°F (around 175°C).

2. Using an immersion blender, blender, or food processor, blend together all ingredients except for the berries.

3. Then carefully stir in your berries.

4. Bake in a loaf pan (preferably silicone) for 40–45 minutes, or until a knife inserted into the middle comes out clean.

ROSEMARY & SAFFRON ORGANIC WHEY PROTEIN BREAD

I almost crushed my head against the ceiling levitating in pleasure when I ate this bread. Not only was it absurdly delicious, it also powered an incredible gym sesh. This is protein powder baking at its finest! Welcome to the party, can I take your coat? Please, take a seat; the BCAAs are in the pitcher, help yourself to some protein cakes. Would you like to try a slice of this ridiculously tasty protein bread too? It just came out of the oven. Ah, follow me, please. ;-)))))))

SERVINGS
1 loaf
NUTRITIONAL DATA PER 1/10 LOAF
50.75kcals, 4.41g protein, 6.1g carbs, 0.8g fat, 1.25g fiber

INGREDIENTS
1 cup liquid egg whites

1/2 cup saffron water (boiling water left to cool with
     a couple strands of saffron)

1/2 cup organic whey protein powder (plain, unsweetened)

1 cup rolled oats (gluten-free or regular)

2 tablespoons chestnut flour

1 tablespoon dried (or freshly chopped!) rosemary

1 tablespoon coconut flour

1 teaspoon baking soda

DIRECTIONS

1. Preheat oven to 325°F (around 160°C).

2. Using an immersion blender, blender, or food processor, blend together all ingredients.

3. Pour into a loaf pan—ideally silicone.

4. Bake for 35–45 minutes, or until a knife inserted into the middle comes out clean.

SUPER BERRY GLUTEN-FREE PROTEIN BREAD

Welcome to a recipe for a sweet berry loaf that's going to revolutionize your breakfasts. Spread one or two slices of this baby right here with a bit of grass-fed butter on top and a side of espresso, and you've got yourself a perfect pre-workout breakfast. If your taste buds are anything like mine, they're going to love this one. :-)

SERVINGS
1 loaf
NUTRITIONAL DATA PER 1/10 LOAF
76kcals, 8.6g protein, 8.5g carbs, 0.9g fat, 1.1g fiber

INGREDIENTS

1 cup unflavored or vanilla pea protein powder

1/2 cup instant buckwheat

1/4 cup dried mulberries

1 cup coconut milk

1 1/2 teaspoons stevia

1/2 teaspoon baking powder

1/2 cup goji berries

1/2 cup frozen blueberries

DIRECTIONS

1. Preheat oven to 350˚F (around 175˚C).

2. Using an immersion blender, blender, or food processor, blend together all ingredients except for the goji berries and blueberries.

3. Once smooth, carefully stir in the berries. (I do this to retain their texture and to prevent my loaf from turning completely purple!)

4. Bake in a loaf pan (preferably silicone) for about 40 minutes, or until a knife inserted into the middle comes out clean.

BANANA PROTEIN BREAD

I think that all too often we find ourselves using the same ingredients, making the same foods, and relying on the same cooking methods. Sure, tried-and-tested recipes and techniques cannot be cast aside in favor of raw experimentation on a daily basis. But every once in a while, when we go out on a limb and try new ingredients, we expand the boundaries of our repertoire, and, oh! incredible things happen!

Let me start with wattleseeds. I've used wattleseeds in my cooking before, and a lot of people emailed me to ask, "What is THAT?" So let me tell you: wattleseeds come from acacia, a type of tree/shrub native to Australia. They are commonly sold ground as a powder, which goes incredibly well with all things chocolate, toffee, and coffee because it has a very nutty—almost hazelnutty—flavor.

You can get wattleseeds in Australia, obviously, but they are available elsewhere, too, in health food stores and online.

What happens if you simply cannot (or do not want to) get wattleseeds? You can use a mixture of cinnamon and chicory powder instead (chicory powder is sold as a coffee substitute in a lot of health food stores). The flavor won't be the same, of course, but you'll still get that sweet and spicy element.

This recipe has three cups of egg whites. Eating a slice of this banana bread is like eating an egg white omelet with a couple of thin slices of banana, half a prune, a tablespoon of raw coconut, and a shot of a protein shake. This makes it a fantastic pre-workout snack to have alongside a tall cup of coffee, and I heartily, oh so heartily, recommend you bring this bread into your world. :-)

SERVINGS
10 slices
NUTRITIONAL DATA PER 1/10 LOAF
94.2kcals, 13.4g protein, 6.8g carbs, 1.03g fat, 1.83g fiber

INGREDIENTS
3 cups liquid egg whites (yes, 3 cups!)

2 small bananas or 1 big one

1/2 cup vanilla or unflavored pea, rice, or a blend of vegan protein powders

2 tablespoons coconut flour

1 tablespoon ground wattleseeds (or a mixture of cinnamon and chicory)

9 whole pitted prunes (or dates if you don't like prunes)

DIRECTIONS
1. Preheat oven to 350°F (around 175°C).

2. Blend together all the ingredients with a blender or food processor.

3. Bake in a loaf pan (preferably silicone) for 40–45 minutes, or until a knife inserted into the middle comes out clean.

I HAVE PUBLISHED A LOT OF WHAT I THINK ARE MUST-TRY RECIPES AT PROTEINPOW. COM—MOST OF THEM ARE NOW IN THIS BOOK!

They're the ones that have yielded jaw-dropping, finger-licking, tear-shedding results. You can tell which recipes are a solid ten out of ten because they are full of exclamation marks, capital letters, and a ridiculous amount of superlatives. Take, for example, this recipe. If the name doesn't give away how much I like it, I don't know what will. I ferociously recommend you try it.

THE ABSOLUTELY AMAZING HEAVEN-DROPPED BURIED-BANANA WHEY PROTEIN BREAD

SERVINGS

1 loaf

NUTRITIONAL DATA PER 1/10 LOAF

96kcals, 8.1g protein, 12.1g carbs, 1.3g fat, 3.2g fiber

INGREDIENTS

1/2 cup pumpkin puree

1/2 cup vanilla whey protein powder

1 cup liquid egg whites

2 bananas (one for the bread batter and
　　　another to bury inside it)

1/2 cup coconut flour

6 tablespoons rolled oats (gluten-free or regular)

1 teaspoon cinnamon

DIRECTIONS

1. Preheat oven to 350°F (around 175°C).

2. Using an immersion blender, blender, or food processor, blend together all ingredients except the second banana.

3. Pour the batter into a loaf pan (preferably silicone) and bury a banana horizontally inside the batter.

4. Bake for 40–60 minutes, or until a knife inserted into the middle (or wherever you're not going to hit the hidden banana) comes out clean.

PROTEIN BANANA BREAD GONE BANANAS

I love adding banana-flavored whey to a banana-containing batter. It gives banana breads an ultra-banana flavor that I think is sensational. I adore bananas—can you tell? If you want less banananess, though, you could always just use a vanilla (or even an unflavored) whey protein powder. I leave it up to your taste buds.

SERVINGS

1 loaf

NUTRITIONAL DATA PER 1/10 LOAF

105kcals, 7.85g protein, 8.79g carbs, 3.98g fat, 1.93g fiber

INGREDIENTS

2 bananas

2 tablespoons coconut flour

3 eggs

2 egg whites

1/2 cup rolled oats (gluten-free or regular)

1/2 cup banana whey protein powder

1/2 cup milk

8 Brazil nuts (I added these for kicks; you can throw in any nut you want—they add a nice flavor and crunch)

1/2 teaspoon baking powder

DIRECTIONS

1. Preheat oven to 325°F (around 160°C).

2. Mix together all the ingredients with a blender or food processor.

3. Bake in a loaf pan (preferably silicone) for 40–45 minutes, or until a knife inserted into the middle comes out clean.

Consider adding a handful of walnuts to the mix before baking! Because banana bread + walnuts = mmmmm. You can also stick a banana down the center of this bread, kind of like my Buried-Banana Whey Protein Bread on page 71. Although . . . well . . . that might be banana overkill if you're using banana whey AND bananas PLUS a buried banana—I mean, we're not monkeys, are we?

CHOCOLATE & WALNUT PROTEIN MINI CAKE LOAVES

SERVINGS

8 mini loaves or jumbo cupcakes

NUTRITIONAL DATA PER MINI LOAF

132kcals, 8g protein, 11g carbs, 5.8g fat, 4.6g fiber

INGREDIENTS

1 egg

1 banana

1 small cooked beet

1/2 cup chocolate hemp protein powder

1 cup coconut milk

1/2 cup rolled oats (gluten-free or regular)

1 tablespoon cocoa powder

1 tablespoon coconut flour

1 teaspoon baking soda

1/2 teaspoon mace powder

1/4 cup goji berries

1/4 cup walnuts

Greek yogurt, optional (for serving)

DIRECTIONS

1. Preheat oven to 350°F (around 175°C).

2. In a blender or food processor, blend together all the ingredients except for the goji berries, walnuts, and Greek yogurt. Once smooth, carefully stir in the berries and nuts.

3. Bake in small loaf pans (preferably silicone) for 40–50 minutes, or until a knife inserted into the middle comes out clean.

4. Top with Greek yogurt, if using.

WHEN I MADE THIS BREAD, I HAD A COUPLE OF SLICES WITH SOME SHARP CHEDDAR ON TOP AND OY! WHAT A SENSATION!

I seriously recommend you try it with the cheddar on top, because there's something about the sharpness of the cheese against the subtle sweetness of the bread that is madness! The bread is also super moist and wholesome and packed full of goodness! What's not to love?

SWEET-OH-SWEET GOJI BERRY PROTEIN BREAD

SERVINGS
16 slices

NUTRITIONAL DATA PER SERVING
53.6kcals,. 5.87g protein, 5g carbs, 1g fat, 2g fiber

INGREDIENTS

1 cup liquid egg whites

1/2 cup unflavored pea protein powder

2 tablespoons buckwheat flour (or oat flour)

2 tablespoons date syrup (or agave)

1/4 cup rolled oats (gluten-free or regular)

1/4 cup omega-3 seeds (a mixture of pumpkin seeds, sunflower seeds, and flaxseed)

2 tablespoons goji berries

DIRECTIONS

1. Preheat oven to 325˚F (around 160˚C).

2. In a blender or food processor, mix together all the ingredients except for the goji berries. Once smooth, carefully stir in the goji berries.

3. Bake in a loaf pan (preferably silicone) for 40–50 minutes, or until a knife inserted into the middle comes out clean. Slice very thin.

PROTEIN
MUFFINS
CUPCAKES

WHAT KIND OF AWARD DID THESE MUFFINS WIN?

They won the Best Protein Muffins of the Year Award.

When? Just now.

Who gave it to them? Me.

Have you made a lot of protein muffins? Ohhhh, have I ever!

How do you know that you won't make even better protein muffins this year? I just know. ;-)

How, though? Because these muffins are 100 percent perfect—in taste, texture, moistness, consistency, lightness, and macros! They just can't be beaten.

How did you come up with the recipe? In other words, why melon? I just saw a melon inside my fridge and thought, "What if . . ." I love melon, you see. It's such a wonder fruit! High in fiber, vitamin B6, folate, vitamin C, vitamin A, etc., and absolutely delicious!

Were you planning on making muffins from the beginning? As a matter of fact, I wasn't. First I thought I'd bake a cake, but I baked some protein quinoa muffins instead. They were all right, but I thought I could do better, so I sketched out a plan for protein cupcakes.

Oh, so you were going to make protein cupcakes? Yes. But I changed my mind when these muffins came out of the oven, because, Zeus, they are PERFECT! They don't really need any frosting.

What do you think will happen to other people when they try this recipe? They're going to flip out.

Flip out how? Well, it depends. Some people may scream and summon their God, while others will simply close their eyes and levitate in bliss; some may scream a mighty "MAMA MIA!" and strike their fist against a table, while others may experience their nom-gasm in silence. I don't know—it really does depend on the person.

Can I have the recipe? Sure can. :-)

ANNA'S AWARD-WINNING PROTEIN MUFFINS

SERVINGS

7 muffins

NUTRITIONAL DATA PER SERVING

106.7kcals, 12.7g protein, 9.8g carbs, 1.55g fat, 3.1g fiber

INGREDIENTS

1/4 cup vanilla whey protein powder

1 cup liquid egg whites

1/4 cup vanilla brown rice protein powder

1/2 fresh melon (cantaloupe), cubed

1 teaspoon baking powder

1/2 cup rolled oats (gluten-free or regular)

DIRECTIONS

1. Preheat oven to 325˚F (about 160˚C).

2. Using an immersion blender or food processor, blend together all ingredients.

3. Pour into six or seven muffin cups and bake for 35–40 minutes, or until a knife inserted into the middle comes out clean.

4. Top them with a tiny bit of organic grass-fed butter when they come out of the oven, and oh! Protein life doesn't get any better than that! :-)))))))

GIANT CHOCOLATE PROTEIN MUFFINS

The other day, I went to watch the movie *Gravity*. Have you seen it? It's a pretty good movie. My only criticism is that it didn't rattle my soul. I thought it'd make a strong point about the wackiness of humanity and how we're all just creatures with an expiration date stamped on our hearts. But it didn't. I mean, not really. Instead, it delivered ninety minutes of terror combined with thrills and a hell of a lot of suspense (the guy next to me was on the verge of chewing both his hands off from the tension). That, combined with the jaw-dropping visuals and truly astounding imagery of space, made the movie totally worth watching. Even if it didn't shake the rug beneath my own sense of reality, it was fine entertainment.

I'm not telling all this because I've always wanted to be a movie critic and now—"Mwa-ha-ha! I get to impose my reviews on a captive audience I've lured here by the promise of a recipe!" No. (Okay . . . maybe a little?)

I'm telling you all this because I made these muffins to eat in the movie theater while I watched *Gravity*. I sneaked them in, tried to unsuccessfully unwrap them without making too much noise (because I stupidly used tinfoil instead of plastic wrap), and nervously munched through what was left of my muffin before handing the other muffin to the right.

SERVINGS

2 large muffins

NUTRITIONAL DATA PER SERVING

245kcals, 27g protein, 21g carbs, 7g fat, 11g fiber

INGREDIENTS

1/4 cup cocoa powder

2 tablespoons coconut flour

1/4 cup brown rice protein powder

1/4 cup chocolate egg white protein powder

2 tablespoons xylitol

1/2 cup almond milk

1/2 teaspoon baking soda

DIRECTIONS

1. Preheat oven to 325˚F (around 160˚C).

2. Using an immersion blender, mixer, or food processor, blend all the above ingredients together until you get a smooth batter.

3. Divide this batter into two giant muffin cups or four regular-size ones.

4. Bake for about 40 minutes, or until a knife inserted into the middle comes out clean, and . . . voilà! Done.

BLUEBERRY WHEY PROTEIN MUFFINS

I solemnly and sincerely declare that the recipe below, if followed in its entirety, shall bring to your life a batch of exquisite, wholly delicious, and nothing short of heavenly protein muffins. Let me explain why these muffins are so good without relying on ridiculous hyperbole. The pumpkin puree, eggs, and dates, together with milk and the blueberries on top, give the muffins a body similar to British sticky toffee pudding—a body that's moist, almost gooey, and sweet—so that what you end up with is a gorgeously textured muffin with a subtle goji and millet richness to it. Then, as you bite through the top, BOOOOM! The blueberries explode and burst into the filling so that, together with the oozing chocolate, they leave you speechless, wondering how it is that such pleasures are not only possible but also healthy.

I really don't know what else to say, aside from, please, try it. It could honestly not be any easier, and the pleasure factor you get from them is just surreal.

SERVINGS
12 muffins

NUTRITIONAL DATA PER SERVING (WITHOUT THE CHOCOLATE INSIDE, BECAUSE THAT IS OPTIONAL; THEY WERE GORGEOUS WITHOUT IT, TOO)
89kcals, 7.5g protein, 12g carbs, 1.7g fat, 1.4g fiber

INGREDIENTS

1 1/4 cups pumpkin puree

4 egg whites

1 egg

2 tablespoons 100 percent cocoa powder

3 pitted medjool dates

1/2 cup unflavored (or chocolate) whey protein powder

1/2 cup millet flakes (or rolled oats)

1/2 cup goji berries

1/2 cup milk (I use chocolate coconut milk, but any milk will do)

1 tablespoon stevia

1/2 teaspoon baking soda

About 1/3 bar (30g) 90 percent dark chocolate, broken into 12 pieces (optional)

About 1/3 bar (30g) white chocolate, broken into 12 pieces (optional)

DIRECTIONS

1. Preheat oven to 325˚F (around 160˚C).

2. Using an immersion blender or food processor, blend all ingredients together (except for the dark and white chocolates).

3. Pour the mixture into muffin cups and place a few blueberries on top of each.

4. Bake for 30–40 minutes, or until a knife inserted into the middle comes out clean.

5. Stick a piece of dark chocolate and a piece of white chocolate inside each muffin. The chocolate begins melting inside at once, and it's delicious!

CHESTNUT & BLUEBERRY WHEY PROTEIN MUFFINS

A dear friend is coming to tea this evening, and I figured, what better way to enjoy our cups of tea than by breaking into some yummy protein muffins? A recent acquisition—the chestnut flour—was secured after a trip to one of my favorite health food stores in town, where I get most of my ingredients. I walked into the store wanting to get some coconut flour, but right where the coconut flour should have been, a bag of chestnut flour lay impudently, hiding the entire row of coconut flour behind it. Taking that as a sign that I ought to try it, I added it to my basket, and just like that: baraboom, it made it into my cupboard and I made these muffins with it. They came out really tasty! The chestnut flour added a kind of nuttiness to the muffins; it made them heavier and denser, so that, in a way, they ended up a lot like oat-bran muffins, if you know what I mean. When the time came to sample one (because, can one really serve to others something one hasn't tried oneself?), out came my tub of almond butter. I opened the drawer, took out a knife, sliced a muffin, and . . . oh, nom, nom, nom, nom. :-)))

SERVINGS
6 or 7 muffins

NUTRITIONAL DATA PER SERVING
98kcals, 9g protein, 14g carbs, 1.3g fat, 3g fiber

INGREDIENTS
1/2 cup chestnut flour

1 cup liquid egg whites

2 tablespoons apple fiber (or flaxseed)

1/2 cup organic whey protein powder

1/2 cup quinoa flakes

1/4 cup applesauce

1 tablespoon stevia

1/2 cup blueberries

DIRECTIONS
1. Preheat oven to 325˚F (around 160˚C).

2. Using an immersion blender, blender, or food processor, blend together all ingredients (except for the blueberries, which you add AFTER blending the rest of the ingredients).

3. Pour into six or seven muffin cups (ideally silicone) and bake for 35–45 minutes, or until a knife inserted into the middle comes out clean.

BANANA PROTEIN CUPCAKES

These cupcakes are GREAT for breakfast, especially next to a big ole cup of coffee. They're banana-y, soft, perfectly moist, and deliver one hell of a protein kaPOW! And to make them, all you need are seven ingredients and thirty minutes of your time. ;-) Here's the recipe:

SERVINGS
4 cupcakes
NUTRITIONAL DATA PER SERVING
250kcals, 24.1g protein, 16g carbs, 8.75g fat, 4.1g fiber

INGREDIENTS
MUFFIN INGREDIENTS
3 tablespoons oat flour

2 large eggs

2 ripe bananas

2 tablespoons coconut flour

1/2 cup banana casein protein powder and whey protein powder blend

FROSTING INGREDIENTS
1/2 cup quark, Greek yogurt, or low-fat ricotta cheese

1/4 cup vanilla or banana casein protein powder

DIRECTIONS
1. Preheat oven to 325˚F (around 160˚C).

2. Using an immersion blender, blender, or food processor, blend all the muffin ingredients together and pour into four muffin cups (preferably silicone).

3. Bake for 30–35 minutes, or until a knife inserted into the middle comes out clean. Remove them from the oven and let them cool.

4. For your frosting, mix quark, Greek yogurt, or low-fat ricotta cheese with the protein powder until you get a creamy frosting.

5. Frost the muffins, sprinkle some cinnamon on top, and . . . voilà! Delicious Banana Protein Cupcakes!

VANILLA & ALMOND PROTEIN MUFFINS

I made these muffins for my friends Mark and Katie, who were driving up to Colorado from New Mexico. I left one out for me to have for breakfast, so I could try them, and I was really happy with the result. The medjool dates inside the muffins add a great texture and an extra level of sweetness that goes really well with the vanilla casein. I spoke with Mark and Katie when they got to Colorado, and it turns out that, between them, they ate all ten muffins on the road! So I reckon it means they liked them, too. :-)

SERVINGS
11 muffins
NUTRITIONAL DATA PER SERVING
81kcals, 8g protein, 4g carbs, 4g fat

INGREDIENTS
1/2 cup applesauce

1/2 cup vanilla casein protein powder

2 tablespoons almond butter

1/2 cup ground almonds

1/4 cup coconut flour

1 cup almond milk

1 tablespoon vanilla extract

3 eggs

1 teaspoon baking powder

6 dates, halved, or walnuts (optional)

DIRECTIONS
1. Preheat oven to 350°F (around 160°C).

2. Using an immersion blender, blender, or food processor, mix all ingredients and pour into muffin cups.

3. Optional: Stick half a date or a walnut inside each one (you could stick a piece of dark chocolate in there, too, or just keep them plain).

4. Bake for 30–35 minutes, or until a knife inserted into the middle comes out clean. :-)

EVERY ONCE IN A WHILE, ON THE PROTEIN POW FACEBOOK PAGE, I LIKE TO PLAY A GAME CALLED "PICK THE NEXT RECIPE!" A GAME WHERE FACEBOOK USERS VOTE ON WHAT THEY WANT ME TO MAKE NEXT.

I give them six options, and I always like to throw in a wildcard—an option that's totally out there, for both the voters and me. This time, the wildcard was "a Protein Cookie Monster (without the cookies)" and lo and behold: it won! So I was left with the challenge of actually creating it. :-D After going through dozens of potential ways to do it, I settled on muffins. My original plan was to bake protein muffins and then cover them completely in blue frosting before adding some eyes and a mouth to the whole thing. But . . . but then I thought that'd look absurd, and would I want to eat that? So I settled on traditional protein cupcakes of a light Cookie-Monstrous shade of blue. ;-)

The recipe for these is extremely simple and involves three steps: (1) make some chocolate protein muffins; (2) make blue protein frosting; (3) frost the muffins. Boom.

COOKIE-MONSTROUS CHOCOLATE CUPCAKES

SERVINGS

7 cupcakes

NUTRITIONAL DATA PER SERVING

207.9kcals, 26.75g protein, 16.6g carbs, 3.5g fat, 5.2g fiber

INGREDIENTS

MUFFIN INGREDIENTS

1 1/4 cups cooked black beans, rinsed and drained

2 eggs

1/2 cup chocolate whey protein powder

1/4 cup chocolate pea protein powder

3/4 tablespoon toffee or vanilla sweetener

2 medium-size cooked (boiled or steamed) beets

1 heaping tablespoon cocoa powder

FROSTING INGREDIENTS

1/2 cup Greek yogurt

1/4 cup vanilla protein powder

1/2 teaspoon blue food coloring (this is optional, but if
you want to make them bright blue, essential)

DIRECTIONS

1. Preheat oven to 325°F (around 160°C).

2. Using an immersion blender, blender, or food
   processor, blend together all the muffin ingredients.

3. Bake for 30–35 minutes, or until a knife inserted into
   the middle comes out clean.

4. After you take them out of the oven, allow the muffins
   to cool.

5. Meanwhile, make your frosting by mixing the frosting
   ingredients together in a bowl. Add food coloring until
   you're happy with the frosting's shade of blue.

6. Once the muffins have cooled, frost them using a
   piping bag or a plastic bag with a corner cut off.

The final product is these protein-PACKED chocolatey cupcakes with a toffee-ness that's just mmmmmmm! Very tasty! And check out the winning macros, too!

BANANA-BUTTERSCOTCH PROTEIN CUPCAKES

There's nothing complicated about making protein cupcakes. It's child's play—so easy. It takes no time for you to end up with a delicious, creamy cupcake that you can sprinkle with coconut flakes, nuts, cinnamon, or cocoa, and/or drizzle with melted chocolate or nut butter! It's protein baking at its finest. :-D

SERVINGS
6 cupcakes
NUTRITIONAL DATA PER SERVING
155kcals, 24g protein, 7g carbs, 4g fat

INGREDIENTS
MUFFIN INGREDIENTS
1/4 cup banana whey protein powder
1 large ripe banana
2 tablespoons sorghum (or oat flour)
2 tablespoons coconut flour
1/4 cup pea protein powder
1 1/2 cups liquid egg whites
1 1/2 teaspoons butterscotch extract

FROSTING INGREDIENTS
1 cup Greek yogurt
3 tablespoons casein protein powder

DIRECTIONS

1. Preheat oven to 350°F (around 175°C).

2. Using an immersion blender, blender, or food processor, blend together all the muffin ingredients and pour into six cupcake cups.

3. Bake for 25–30 minutes, or until a knife inserted into the middle comes out clean. Pay attention not to overbake them, because then they'll turn out dry!

4. Take them out as soon as they are cooked through. Then let them cool.

5. While they are cooling, make your frosting by mixing the frosting ingredients.

6. Frost each muffin, using a piping bag or a plastic bag with the corner cut off, to transform it into—ta-daaaa!—a delicious homemade protein cupcake! I drizzled peanut butter on top, and it brought the whole thing together beautifully, so I highly recommend it. If, however, you want to keep your cupcakes nut-free, just omit the PB and add some melted dark chocolate, instead!

PROTEIN MUFFINS WITH A CHOCOLATE CASEIN FILLING

SERVINGS
9 muffins
NUTRITIONAL DATA FOR FULL RECIPE
160kcals, 20.4g protein, 11.4g carbs, 4.7g fat, 3.8g fiber

I made this recipe eggless, just to show you that, if you prefer to bake without eggs, you can do just fine without them. ;-) I also threw in a bunch of pistachios because, well . . . I love pistachios. The final muffins were super moist inside, and together with the creamy casein filling, they basically just explode in your mouth with a vanilla-chocolatey pumpkin-packed kaBOOOM! The apple, banana, and pumpkin lend the muffins a lot of umph—texture-wise—while upping the muffins' nutritional profile several notches. Something else I really liked about these was the cocoa on top, because since it's plain 100 percent cocoa, it offsets the sweetness of the casein protein powder really nicely.

INGREDIENTS

MUFFIN INGREDIENTS
1 small apple, cored and peeled

1/2 cup vanilla whey protein powder

1 banana

1 1/4 cups pumpkin puree

1/2 cup rolled oats (gluten-free or regular)

2 tablespoons chia seeds, plus extra for sprinkling on top

1/4 cup coconut milk (or almond milk)

1/4 cup pistachios

100 percent organic cocoa powder for sprinkling on top

FILLING INGREDIENTS
1/2 cup chocolate casein protein powder

3/4 cup milk (almond, coconut, or regular milk)

DIRECTIONS

1. Preheat oven to 325°F (around 160°C).

2. Using an immersion blender, blender, or food processor, blend together all the muffin ingredients, except the cocoa powder.

3. Spoon batter into nine silicone muffin cups.

4. Bake for 30–35 minutes, or until a knife inserted into the middle comes out clean.

5. Once the muffins have cooled, scoop out their centers (save those for later snacking).

6. Mix together the filling ingredients and, using either a piping bag or a plastic bag with the corner cut off, squeeze the filling into the muffins.

7. Sprinkle on top the final touches: 100 percent organic cocoa powder and some extra chia seeds.

8. Bake for 10–12 minutes. Keep an eye on them after 10 minutes and remove them from the oven as soon as they've cooked through.

MY NEW MEXICAN CHOCOLATE PROTEIN MUFFINS

When I visit northern New Mexico in the late summer and I find myself at an altitude of 7,000 feet, I feel like I'm in heaven. Instead of going to the gym, I just go outside for a jog or use my TRX. It is so gorgeous there—so peaceful! Yes, it gets quite hot in the summer, but the heat there is dry and bearable. It's not like it is in England, where anything above 80˚F makes you feel like you're going to self-combust. In northern New Mexico you can just sit out like an iguana, absorbing the rays, as you take in the breathtakingly beautiful landscape of the green mountains all around you. Anyway, before I break into a proper "Visit New Mexico" commercial, let me give you this recipe. It contains a secret ingredient you may not readily associate with muffins: black beans. Yup. Black beans. I mean, I'm in New Mexico—I have to make something with one of the state's most popular foods. ;-)

SERVINGS
11 muffins

NUTRITIONAL DATA PER SERVING
82kcals, 8g protein, 6g carbs, 3g fat, 4g fiber

INGREDIENTS
1 1/4 cups cooked black beans, rinsed and drained

1/2 cup chocolate or mocha cappuccino whey protein powder

4 tablespoons coconut flour

1/2 cup coconut milk

3 eggs

1/4 cup cocoa powder

1/4 cup sucralose, stevia, or xylitol

DIRECTIONS

1. Preheat oven to 350˚F (around 175˚C).

2. Using an immersion blender, blender, or food processor, blend the above ingredients together.

3. Pour into eleven muffin cups (preferably silicone).

4. Bake for 20–25 minutes, or until a knife inserted into the middle comes out clean. You don't want to overcook them, because they'll dry out if you do, so make sure you remove them from the oven as SOON as they're cooked through.

5. When they're ready, let them cool and eat them solo or top them with protein frosting, Greek yogurt, or nut butter!

A PEANUT BUTTER LOVER'S MUFFIN DREAM

This might be one of the best things I've ever made with protein powder.

I took my first bite, and I swear I died a little. The world around me faded. The birds stopped singing. My kitchen disappeared. All I saw was this muffin, and all I tasted was peanut butter. My heart almost exploded.

How would I describe it? It's . . . ridiculous. The whole concept! It's . . . audacious. The result is spectacular . . . SUPREME! It's a peanut butter lover's DELIGHT.

SERVINGS
3 muffins
NUTRITIONAL DATA PER MUFFIN
295kcals, 36.8g protein, 11.7g carbs, 11.7g fat, 6.4g fiber

INGREDIENTS

1/2 cup vanilla or peanut butter and
    marshmallow whey protein powder
1 cup liquid egg whites
2 tablespoons buckwheat flour
1/4 cup coconut flour
3 Peanut Butter & Marshmallow Protein Cups (page 170)

DIRECTIONS

1. Preheat oven to 350˚F (around 175˚C).

2. Using an immersion blender, blender, or food processor, blend everything together (except for the peanut butter cups).

3. Fill three muffin cups halfway with batter and top with a peanut butter cup, then fill up the muffin cups with the remaining batter.

4. Bake for about 15 minutes, or until a knife inserted into the middle comes out relatively clean.

5. Let the muffins cool before removing from the cups to ensure the chocolate from your peanut butter cup doesn't stick to the sides. That, my dear protein babies, is IT.

VANILLA & BANANA PROTEIN MUFFINS

"Pa, I want you to make me some eggs for breakfast . . . do NOT forget about THE BUTTER!" That's how I used to request, scrap that, DEMAND my eggs for breakfast—always served with melted butter on top. This was as a child, because, as I "teenaged up" and started growing a dietary conscience, the "evils" of butter were authoritatively brought to the fore by our "beloved" media, so that butter = unhealthy = saturated fats = heart disease = horror = grrrr = boo-hoo-hoo. It's only recently that butter's blameless smile has begun shining under the spotlight (I'm here speaking of the organic kind), and butter = lecithin, selenium, and vitamins A, K, D, and E. While I don't engage in the consumption of butter by the cupful, I often like adding a layer to my (protein) toast, a square to my (protein) pancakes, a tablespoon to some cakes. Though most of the time I completely forget about butter (after years of relegating it to the domain of the "no, thank you"), sometimes I remember and in it goes. That is what happened here, and notice the macros: nothing insalubrious and one hell of a taste boom.

INGREDIENTS

1/2 cup liquid egg whites
1/2 cup quinoa flakes
2 tablespoons coconut flour (or ground almonds)
2 teaspoons vanilla pea protein powder
2 teaspoons vanilla casein protein powder
2 tablespoons vanilla whey protein powder
2 tablespoons Greek yogurt
1 tablespoon butter
1/2 cup milk (I use coconut milk)
1/2 banana
9 walnuts, for the top
Butter, for topping

DIRECTIONS

1. Preheat oven to 325˚F (around 160˚C).

2. Using an immersion blender, blender, or food processor, blend the above ingredients together—except the walnuts and the butter. Fill muffin cups with batter.

3. Bake for 25–35 minutes, or until a knife inserted into the middle comes out relatively clean.

4. Top with butter! This is optional but absolutely lovely.

SERVINGS
9 muffins
NUTRITIONAL DATA PER SERVING
89kcals, 7g protein, 5.8g carbs, 3.8g fat, 2g fiber

YOU PROBABLY DON'T KNOW THIS ABOUT ME, BUT I'M A HUUUUGE MOVIE BUFF.

I derive extreme amounts of pleasure from getting to the theater exceptionally early, picking a good seat (halfway in, behind a short person), watching the previews (inwardly heckling the bad ones), and then . . . when the movie starts, quietly opening my bag and taking out my homemade snack.

I don't know why, I've just always had a thing for making my own snacks and sneaking them into movie theaters. There's something fun about digging into something tasty as you watch all kinds of madness on the big screen. I mean, that's why popcorn is so popular, at the end of the day! But movie popcorn is not really an ideal snack, not to me, especially not the flavored kind available at most movie theaters.

And the options available are pretty so-so—there's hot dogs, nachos, chocolates, and candy. Quite frankly, those have never, ever appealed to me. Who wants to eat a hot dog or nachos, sauce silently dripping all over the place? Or mindlessly go through a whole box of sugar and calories in a matter of seconds? Beh. I've never been a fan.

That's why I bring my own snacks, even though my friends always laugh at them. ;-) "Anna, I can't believe you brought chicken breasts to the movie theater! And that you sat next to Vanessa!" (one of our vegetarian friends) or "Is that a . . . box of puffed rice cereal!?" or "Those aren't pancakes, are they?" But what's one to do? There aren't that many options AT the movie theater!

That's why I made these mini muffins! To enjoy in the movie theater while I watched *Les Misérables*. :-)

MINI BLUEBERRY PROTEIN MUFFINS

SERVINGS

15 mini muffins

NUTRITIONAL DATA PER SERVING

22.86kcals, 2.7g protein, 1.6g carbs, 0.42g fat, 1.2g fiber

INGREDIENTS

1/2 cup liquid egg whites

1/4 cup rolled oats (gluten-free or regular)

1/4 cup vanilla whey protein powder

1 tablespoon coconut flour

1 teaspoon xylitol (optional)

1/2 teaspoon baking powder

2 tablespoons cottage cheese (cooked sweet potato or banana would also work!)

15 blueberries

DIRECTIONS

1. Preheat oven to 325˚F (around 160˚C).

2. Using an immersion blender, blender, or food processor, blend the above ingredients together—except the blueberries. Pour into fifteen mini muffin cups, with a single blueberry on top. I made them using a mini muffin silicone mold. If you don't have one, you can use regular muffin tins instead and just bake the muffins for a bit longer.

3. Bake for 10–15 minutes, or until a knife inserted into the middle comes out clean.

4. Once they're ready, let them cool, eat a couple of them, and pack the rest in a plastic bag to take with you to the movie theater and munch through the main feature—wooooo!!!!

SWEET POTATO & VANILLA PROTEIN CAKES WITH VANILLA CASEIN FILLING

Whenever you see a recipe—mine or somebody else's—using cooked sweet potatoes, remember you can replace them with cooked pumpkin (pumpkin puree or actual cooked fresh pumpkin) or cooked butternut squash. The flavor will differ slightly (with pumpkin a tiny bit more tart, potatoes a tiny bit sweeter, and butternut squash a tiny bit nuttier), but whatever you're making is bound to be equally good.

SERVINGS
8 mini cakes or muffins

NUTRITIONAL DATA PER SERVING
112.9kcals. 13.2g protein, 6.5g carbs, 2.2g fat, 1.5g fiber

INGREDIENTS

MUFFIN INGREDIENTS
3/4 cup quark or cottage cheese (or ricotta or mascarpone)

3/4 cup liquid egg whites

2 medium-size cooked sweet potatoes

1/2 cup vanilla whey protein powder

2 tablespoons coconut flour

1 tablespoon vanilla extract

1 1/2 teaspoons cinnamon

FROSTING INGREDIENTS
1/2 cup vanilla casein protein powder

1/2 cup coconut milk

DIRECTIONS

1. Preheat oven to 325°F (around 160°C).

2. Using an immersion blender, blender, or food processor, blend together all the muffin ingredients.

3. Bake in eight mini cake pans or muffin cups (preferably silicone) for about 35 minutes, or until a knife inserted into the middle comes out clean.

4. When your cakes cool, slice them all horizontally and fill them with a casein protein powder frosting made by mixing the casein protein powder and milk.

5. Stack the top layers on top of the bottom layers.

CHOCOLATE, PUMPKIN & PASSION FRUIT PROTEIN CAKES

"I'll bring the dessert!" I said as we put the final touches on our plan to meet for dinner with a couple of dear and darling friends. Because of my proclivity for last-minuteness, I didn't decide on what exactly I'd be making until the morning of the dinner itself. My goal was to make something jam-packed with flavor, something lush, something both super-healthy and super-sumptuous—something with protein powder that our non-powder-eating, veggie-loving friends would love. Welcome to these Chocolate, Pumpkin & Passion Fruit Protein Cakes!

SERVINGS

9 mini cakes or muffins

NUTRITIONAL DATA PER SERVING

94.4kcals, 10g protein, 13g carbs, 2g fat, 3g fiber

INGREDIENTS

1/2 cup liquid egg whites

1/2 cup pumpkin puree

1 passion fruit, scooped

1/2 cup vanilla brown rice protein powder

1 cup coconut or almond milk

1/2 cup millet flakes

2 tablespoons cocoa

1 tablespoon hazelnut butter (or almond butter)

1 1/2 teaspoons baking soda

9 medjool dates

DIRECTIONS

1. Preheat oven to 325°F (around 160°C).

2. Using an immersion blender, blender, or food processor, blend together all ingredients, except the dates.

3. Pour into a mini cake loaf pan or into muffin cups.

4. Bake for 25–35 minutes, or until a knife inserted into the middle comes out clean.

5. When dessert time rolls around, dig a little hole into each mini lad and insert a pitted medjool date inside. Result? KAPOOOOW! Deliciousness.

BANANA & PUMPKIN WHEY PROTEIN MUFFINS

I love making these muffins when we're having our friends over or when we go to a party, especially with a layer of peanut or almond butter in between. They're just a great way to introduce people to protein powder foods and show them how great protein baking can be!

SERVINGS
8 muffins
NUTRITIONAL DATA PER MUFFIN
80kcals, 8.5g protein, 7.4g carbs, 1.4g fat, 2.7g fiber

INGREDIENTS
1/2 cup vanilla whey protein powder
1/4 cup pumpkin puree (or cooked sweet potato)
3/4 cup liquid egg whites
1/4 cup low-fat cottage cheese (or Greek yogurt)
1/2 cup rolled oats (gluten-free or regular)
1/4 cup coconut flour
1 banana

DIRECTIONS

1. Preheat oven to 350°F (around 175°C).

2. Blend together all ingredients in a blender or food processor until smooth.

3. Scoop the batter into a muffin tin (ideally silicone). This should make 8 muffins.

4. Bake for 20–25 minutes, or until a knife inserted into one of the muffins comes out clean. Keep an eye on them after 15 minutes and remove them from the oven as soon as your knife comes out clean. Pay attention so you don't overcook them, because if you do, the whey can turn against you and dry out the muffins.

CINNAMON PROTEIN CAKES

I think this recipe is a perfect example of how baking with protein powders does not have to EVER yield rubbery or hm-hm-textured baked goods. It can yield soft, cakey, and super moist breads, cakes, and muffins!

All you have to do is understand the powders and know that you have to properly offset whey and/ or casein protein powder with plenty of wet and heavy ingredients (like milk, eggs, coconut flour, and applesauce!).

Bear in mind that you can follow this recipe and, instead of baking it in a cake pan or mini loaf pan as I did, bake it in muffin cups. Also, consider adding some nuts or seeds to the mixture or eat the cakes with nut butter—mmmm. This will kick the whole experience up several notches and deliver a full-blown protein deliciousness—BAAAAAAM!

SERVINGS
4 mini cakes or muffins
NUTRITIONAL DATA PER SERVING (1/4 RECIPE)
50kcals, 5.5g protein, 2.8g carbs, 2g fat, 1.4g fiber

INGREDIENTS
1/4 cup cinnamon whey and casein protein
    powder blend
2 tablespoons coconut flour
1/4 cup applesauce
1/2 cup coconut milk
2 eggs

DIRECTIONS
1. Preheat oven to 325°F (around 160°C).

2. Using an immersion blender, blender, or food processor, blend together all ingredients.

3. Pour the mixture into four mini loaf pans or four muffin cups.

4. Bake for about 25–35 minutes, or until a knife inserted into the middle comes out clean.

COOKIES & CREAM PROTEIN CUPCAKES

The secret to these cupcakes is in the frosting. All you need to make it is black onyx cocoa powder! Well, that and whey protein powder plus Greek yogurt. That first ingredient may sound exotic to some of you, but it's totally worth finding! I bought it when I was in New Mexico, and as soon as I saw—and tasted it—all I could think of were Oreos! That's how this recipe was born.

SERVINGS

8 cupcakes

NUTRITIONAL DATA PER SERVING

161kcals, 25g protein, 7g carbs, 5g fat

INGREDIENTS

MUFFIN INGREDIENTS

1 banana

1 cup liquid egg whites

1/2 cup chocolate rice protein powder

1/2 cup chocolate pea protein powder

1/4 cup ground flaxseeds

1 cup almond milk

FROSTING INGREDIENTS

1/2 cup Greek yogurt

1/2 cup chocolate whey protein powder

1/4 cup black onyx cocoa powder

DIRECTIONS

1. Preheat oven to 350˚F (around 175˚C).

2. First, make the muffins by blending all the muffin ingredients using an immersion blender, blender, or food processor.

3. Pour the mix into eight to ten silicone muffin cups (depending on their size).

4. Bake for about 35–40 minutes, or until a knife inserted into the middle comes out clean. Set aside muffins to cool.

5. Meanwhile, make your protein frosting by mixing together all the frosting ingredients.

6. Stick the frosting in a piping bag with a nozzle or cut off the corner of a plastic bag.

7. Frost all the muffins to transform them into . . . cupcakes!

PROTEIN
PIZZA
WRAPS
BURGERS

ALMOND & QUINOA-BASED PROTEIN PIZZA

SERVINGS

3 small crusts or 1 large one

**NUTRITIONAL DATA PER CRUST
(IF YOU MAKE 3 SMALL ONES)**

171.3kcals, 14g protein, 13.5g carbs, 6.1g fat, 4.3g fiber

INGREDIENTS

2 tablespoons pea protein powder

2 tablespoons ground almonds

1 tablespoon coconut flour

1/2 cup quinoa flakes (you can replace the quinoa
　　with rolled oats)

1 egg

4 egg whites

2 tablespoons coconut milk

1 teaspoon dried rosemary

1 teaspoon dried thyme

1 teaspoon sea salt

DIRECTIONS

1. Blend all ingredients together.

2. Pan-fry as one giant pancake on a hot, hot, hot
   nonstick pan further nonsticked with a teaspoon
   of coconut oil or some low-calorie cooking
   spray.

3. Add pizza toppings.

4. Stick it under the broiler for 10–15 minutes.

I GREW UP THINKING ANCHOVIES SHOULD NEVER COME ANYWHERE NEAR PIZZA.

I blame the Ninja Turtles for this. It took me ages to find out that anchovies on pizza are actually quite good (something about their saltiness against the sweetness of the tomato sauce . . . mmmmm!). Another controversial "you either love it or hate it" pizza topping is pineapple. Just as I did with anchovies, I used to violently shun pineapple on pizza—I thought it was an abomination, a bona fide defilement of good taste. That all changed one night when my friend Kim and I decided to order a pizza. We quickly found ourselves in the middle of a standoff. On one end, there I was voicing argument after argument against the placement of pineapple on pizza ("I will have NONE of it!"). On the other end, Kim (a pineapple-on-pizza lover) stood her ground, threatening me with "I'm ordering it!" and "Try and stop me!" We ended up meeting each other halfway: we ordered half the pizza with pineapple and the other half with extra tomatoes. Then, in the spirit of friendship, I ate one of her slices. That's when I realized that I was a FOOL, because, oh la la! pineapple on pizza! Who knew? Who knew that the texture, juiciness, and sweetness of the pineapple would go so well on pizza? Anyway, if you're wondering why I'm rambling on about this, it's because I want to urge those of you with pizza-topping preconceptions to shed them and try something new. ;-) This pizza crust gives you the chance to do that while enjoying a high-protein, gluten-free, and rich-in-omega-3 pizza crust, so . . . play away! And if you're feeling adventurous, why not try sliced banana on pizza like my Swedish friend Stina does?

QUINOA & FLAXSEED HAWAIIAN PROTEIN PIZZA

SERVINGS

1 pizza crust

**NUTRITIONAL DATA PER SERVING
(WITHOUT TOPPINGS, AS THOSE ARE UP TO YOU)**

212.15kcals, 15.6g protein, 24.9g carbs, 6.15g fat, 5g fiber

INGREDIENTS

CRUST INGREDIENTS

1 cup liquid egg whites

1/2 cup unflavored pea, rice, or other
vegan protein powder blend

1/4 cup quinoa flakes

2 tablespoons flaxseeds

1/2 cup almond or, if you can find it,
quinoa milk

BASIC TOPPINGS

Tomato paste or sauce

Cheese (I use about a handful of a
cheddar-mozzarella mix)

Herbs (rosemary, thyme, and basil work
beautifully on pizza!)

Olive oil (optional)

DIRECTIONS

1. First, blend the crust ingredients using a food processor or handheld blender.

2. Spray your nonstick frying pan with some low-calorie cooking spray or coconut oil and turn it to hot.

3. Spread your batter on a nonstick pan and fry it like a big and dense pancake. Take it off the pan (after, of course, flipping it) and add your toppings. I take the lazy person's way out and just use tomato paste from a tube, but if you want to make a nice tomato sauce for the pizza, use that instead. :-)

4. After the tomato sauce, add your toppings, and then cheese and herbs (rosemary, thyme, and basil work beautifully on pizza!). I ended up using about a handful of a cheddar-mozzarella mix.

5. The final step is to throw the whole thing under the broiler for about 10–15 minutes. You can brush some olive oil around the outer edge to ensure it gets crispy. That's it— pizza done.

ANOTHER HAWAIIAN PROTEIN PIZZA

I made this pizza crust using just four ingredients: egg whites, oat flour, extra-virgin olive oil, and pea protein powder. If you don't have pea protein powder, you can replace it with another powder. I've included a few suggestions below. But let me try to build a case for cooking with pea protein powder, okay? Because it's one of the "underdog" protein powders, and it deserves a lot more love than it's currently being given!

Okay. Pea protein powder is naturally savory. It tastes (drumroll . . .) of peas. The first time I tried it, I remember thinking I'd been had, because I followed the tub's directions, which said to mix it with water and drink it like a shake. >:-(I took a sip of this yellow shake thing and "Arrrr, WHAT IS THIS?!" I was REALLY unimpressed. It tasted of food; it tasted of . . . soup. So I did with it what I do with all the protein powders I don't like: I relegated it to the domain of The Forgotten. Then, one day, I thought, hey! Let's try to speak its language. And I started experimenting with the powder—making savory breads, wraps, tortillas, etc.!

SERVINGS

1 crust

NUTRITIONAL DATA PER SERVING

(WITHOUT TOPPINGS, AS THOSE ARE UP TO YOU)

331kcals, 39.6g protein, 19.7g carbs, 2.5g fat, 5g fiber

INGREDIENTS

1/2 cup liquid egg whites

2 teaspoons oat flour (or buckwheat flour)

1 1/2 teaspoons extra-virgin olive oil

1/4 cup unflavored pea protein powder

Toppings of your choice

DIRECTIONS

1. Blend together all the ingredients, except the toppings.

2. Spray a nonstick pan with some low-calorie cooking spray or coconut oil.

3. Get the pan super hot.

4. Pour the batter into the pan and turn the heat to medium. You're basically making a pancake here!

5. Once the first side has cooked, flip it.

6. Remove it from the heat and add your pizza toppings to it, beginning with tomato paste (or ketchup, if you're award-winningly lazy), sliced ham, pineapple, cheese, and whatever herbs you like! I used fresh rosemary and oregano on mine, and it was . . . mmmm: sublime.

7. Once all your toppings are on it, stick it under the broiler until the cheese has melted. You can spray the edges of the pizza with some low-calorie cooking spray or olive oil to make it crunchy, OR if you have a kitchen brush, you can just brush some extra-virgin olive oil on there. That's it, your pizza's ready to be demolished. ;-D

LOW-CARB PROTEIN PIZZA

Here's another recipe for a protein pizza crust, this time featuring onion, rosemary, and thyme. Adding veggies and herbs to your crust is a great way to add flavor to your pizza! And you can add any herbs you like to it—for example, ground (or freshly picked) basil goes great on a mozzarella and tomato pizza, and parsley is fantastic if you're planning on topping your pizza with meat! Just follow your taste buds here and enjoy. :-)

SERVINGS
1 crust
NUTRITIONAL DATA PER SERVING
(WITHOUT TOPPINGS, AS THOSE ARE UP TO YOU)
389kcals, 62.7g protein, 27.7g carbs, 3.1g fat, 17.1g fiber

INGREDIENTS
1 cup liquid egg whites
1/4 cup psyllium husk powder
1/2 cup pea protein powder
1 tablespoon ground rosemary
    and thyme
1 teaspoon onion granules
Toppings of your choice

DIRECTIONS
1. Blend together all the ingredients, except the toppings.

2. Spray a nonstick pan with some low-calorie cooking spray or coconut oil.

3. Get the pan super hot.

4. Pour the batter into the pan, spread it around with a spoon or spatula, and turn the heat to medium.

5. Once the bottom side has cooked, flip it. Imagine you're making a thick pancake here.

OATY PROTEIN PIZZA

This is one of my favorite recipes to make when I'm in a hurry because it's really easy and takes no time at all. It's also very oaty and mmmm! I love it! And I hope you do, too. :-)

SERVINGS
1 crust
NUTRITIONAL DATA PER SERVING
523kcals, 53g protein, 54g carbs, 9g fat

INGREDIENTS

1 cup rolled oats (gluten-free or regular)

1 egg

4 egg whites

1/4 cup unflavored pea protein powder

1/2 teaspoon rosemary

1/2 teaspoon thyme

Salt to taste

Toppings of your choice

DIRECTIONS

1. Blend all ingredients together.

2. Pan-fry as one giant pancake on a hot, hot, hot nonstick pan further nonsticked with a teaspoon of coconut oil or some low-calorie cooking spray.

3. Once it's cooked and looks like a dense protein pancake, remove it from the pan.

4. Add your pizza toppings—beginning with tomato paste, veggies and/or meats, and ending with cheese (ideally mozzarella) and more herbs like basil, thyme, rosemary, or parsley!

5. Stick it under the broiler for 10–15 minutes, or until the cheese melts.

LOW-CARB PROTEIN WRAPS

Protein wraps are one of the best foods you can make with your protein powders! They're easy, quick to make, and you can fill them with all sorts of gorgeous vegetables and meats. Whether you're in the office, school, gym, on the playground, or in the comfort of your own kitchen, when lunchtime strikes, boom! Protein wraps deliver. ;-) I've uploaded quite a few protein wraps on proteinpow.com, as well as tortillas and crepes. I just love them. And there are so many ways you can play around with the flavors and macros.

SERVINGS

3 wraps

NUTRITIONAL DATA PER WRAP

70.1kcals, 9.2g protein, 4.2g carbs, 2g fat, 3g fiber

INGREDIENTS

3 tablespoons organic unflavored whey protein powder

1/2 cup liquid egg whites

1 tablespoon flaxseeds

1 tablespoon psyllium husks

1 teaspoon sea salt

Toppings of your choice

DIRECTIONS

1. Blend everything together, except toppings.

2. Preheat a nonstick pan, further nonsticked with some low-calorie cooking spray or coconut oil.

3. Get the pan HOT, HOT, HOT, and then pour 1/3 of your mixture into it, spreading it around with a spoon and turning the heat down to medium when you do.

4. Spread the mixture in the pan by tilting the pan or using a spatula to spread it. Once you see bubbles begin to form on top, flip your wrap.

5. Then flip it again and set it aside on a plate.

6. Repeat to make the second one and then the third.

7. When they're all ready, let them cool, add your filling on top, and then wrap the whole thing tightly with some aluminum foil. This makes the wrap a lot easier to transport—and to eat, because it ensures nothing falls out the other end (and lands on your wizard's frock . . . ruining it forevah).

THE BEST RED PEPPER LOW-CARB PROTEIN WRAPS IN THE WORLD

I know this will sound odd to you, but these wraps taste a bit like corn tortillas, I don't know why. I absolutely love them though and will be making them again and again and again, because the macros are surreal and the flavor is . . . out of this world!

SERVINGS

3 wraps

NUTRITIONAL DATA PER SERVING

59.4kcals, 7.6g protein, 4.7g carbs, 1.2g fat, 3g fiber

INGREDIENTS

2 tablespoons psyllium husks
2 tablespoons unflavored whey protein powder
1 egg
1 egg white
1 red bell pepper, seeded and chopped
Sea salt to taste

DIRECTIONS

1. Blend everything together.

2. Preheat a nonstick pan, further nonsticked with coconut oil or low-fat spray, and let it get hot.

3. When it gets sizzling hot, spoon about 1/3 of your mixture into the center of the pan and, with a spoon, spread it around.

4. Lower the heat to medium as soon as you've spread the batter. Once it looks like it's cooked on one side, flip it.

5. Do this three times to get three wraps!

FETA-FILLED PROTEIN WRAPS

Someone once asked me to compile a list of my favorite wrap-filling cheeses, and this is what I came up with: (1) feta, (2) buffalo mozzarella, (3) queso panela, (4) anthotiro, (5) mascarpone, (6) sharp English cheddar, (7) Wensleydale, (8) ricotta, (9) Gruyère, and (10) kefalotyri. There are others, of course, but these are my top ten!

These cheeses all vary dramatically in sharpness, texture, and depth of flavor, but they have one thing in common: they're all absolutely delicious in protein wraps! You can also combine them to make insane fillings; mix them with creamy mushrooms or spinach or even add some nuts (walnuts and pine nuts are wonderful) or dried fruits (like cranberries or apricots).

When I'm feeling lazy, though, I usually just use one cheese, and the one I use the most is feta. I just love feta—I love its saltiness and the way it melts, becoming soft and almost creamy. It's gorgeous on salad (hail the Greek salad!), crumbled on veggies, eaten with sweet potato fries (a personal favorite), and it's also gorgeous in protein wraps and quesadillas. ;-)

SERVINGS

2 wraps

NUTRITIONAL DATA PER WRAP

164.8kcals, 22.6g protein, 3.8g carbs, 6.3g fat

INGREDIENTS

1 egg white

2 tablespoons pea protein powder

2 tablespoons milk

Salt, pepper, herbs (optional)

Flaxseeds or hemp seeds (optional)

About 1/4 cup crumbled feta cheese

DIRECTIONS

1. First, blend together all the above ingredients except the feta to form a smooth batter. I use coconut milk, but any milk will do the job here (a hazelnut or almond milk would be lovely!). You can "season" the batter, too, before cooking it—add salt, pepper, herbs, or spices. You can also add flaxseeds or hemp seeds to make your wraps nuttier in flavor and add some nice omega-3 fatty acids to the mix. ;-)

2. Preheat a nonstick pan, further nonsticked with some coconut oil, low-calorie cooking spray, or a bit of butter. Pour batter into hot pan and flip when it is dry on top and looks cooked.

3. When it's cooked through, fill with feta cheese (you can use however much you want). You can make a large one, and just fill it with all the cheese. It's entirely up to you, your level of hunger, and of course, your taste buds. ;-)

THESE TUNA BURGERS CONTAIN NO PROTEIN POWDER BUT ARE NATURALLY FULL OF PROTEIN—KA-POW-POW—NEVERTHELESS.

The burger buns are, however, made with protein. You can make the tuna burgers without the buns, or you can make the buns without the burgers. That, or you can make them for each other, as their creator intended.

Whatever you do, though, just make sure you try these, because they're a great way to eat what is actually a really healthy burger!

TUNA BURGERS WITH PROTEIN POWDER BUNS

SERVINGS
4 burgers with buns

BUN

NUTRITIONAL DATA PER BUN

81.65kcals, 2.5g carbs, 11.15g protein, 2.95g fat, 0.6g fiber

INGREDIENTS

1/4 cup unflavored whey
      protein powder
1/4 cup buckwheat flour
      (or oat flour)
1/2 cup liquid egg whites
1 tablespoon coconut flour
2 tablespoons cottage cheese
      or Greek yogurt
2 tablespoons unflavored
      pea protein powder
1/2 teaspoon baking powder
1/2 teaspooon salt
2 teaspoons sesame seeds (optional)

DIRECTIONS

1. Preheat oven to 325°F (around 160°C). Line a cookie sheet with parchment paper or use a silicone or nonstick cookie sheet.

2. Blend together all bun ingredients except sesame seeds. Make four "buns" on the prepared cookie sheet. You can add some sesame seeds on top before baking for further burger-bun aesthetics.

3. Bake for about 15–20 minutes, or until a knife inserted in the middle comes out clean. Keep an eye out to not overcook them. They won't brown much, so don't wait until they do! Set buns aside to cool. (You could prepare the burgers now, if you like.)

BURGER

NUTRITIONAL DATA PER TUNA BURGER

81.65kcals, 8.6g carbs, 15.1g protein, 1.15g fat, 2.1g fiber

INGREDIENTS

1 red onion, chopped
1 can tuna, in spring water or brine
1 egg
1 tablespoon rolled oats (gluten-free or regular)
1 tablespoon tomato puree
1 teaspoon onion granules
1 teaspoon salt
1 teaspoon paprika
2 teaspoons whole grain mustard
1/2 teaspoon allspice (weird, I know, but it works!)
1/2 teaspoon garlic granules
Optional toppings: ketchup, mayo, mustard, tomato, lettuce
      (or other greens), avocado, sliced sweet potato, cheese, etc.

DIRECTIONS

1. On medium heat, preheat a nonstick pan, further nonsticked with some coconut oil or low-cal spray. Add the onion and sauté it until it's soft and caramelizes a bit. Put onions in a large bowl and wipe out pan.

2. Chuck the rest of the ingredients into the bowl with the onions, and mix everything together with a spoon or fork.

3. Heat the same pan, nonsticked again with coconut oil or spray. Meanwhile, shape four patties out of the mix.

4. When pan is hot, lay the burgers into it. Remember that you want the pan to be sizzling hot when you place the burgers in it. As soon as you do that, though, turn the heat down to medium (just so the bottom "seals up" nicely and then the rest of the burger cooks).

5. Flip the burgers when the bottom side has cooked and gained some color.

6. When the burger is done, slice your buns in half, add your burger, some tomato, lettuce (or other greens), avocado, etc. You can add some sliced sweet potato even or a fried egg and of course ketchup and mayo +/- mustard! You can also throw on some blue cheese or goat's cheese or Gruyère or whatever you like best on your burgers!

BEEF BURGERS WITH PROTEIN POWDER BUNS

SERVINGS
5 burgers with buns

BUN

NUTRITIONAL DATA PER BUN
92kcals, 9g protein, 8g carbs, 3g fat, 2g fiber

INGREDIENTS
1/4 cup unflavored pea protein powder
2 tablespoons rolled oats (gluten-free or regular)
3 tablespoons buckwheat flakes
1/4 cup coconut flour
1 egg
1 egg white
1/2 teaspoon baking soda
2 teaspoons sesame seeds, optional

DIRECTIONS
1. Preheat oven to 325˚ F (around 160˚ C). Line a cookie sheet with parchment paper or use a silicone or nonstick cookie sheet.

2. Blend together all bun ingredients except sesame seeds. Make four "buns" on the prepared cookie sheet. You can add some sesame seeds on top before baking for further burger-bun aesthetics.

3. Bake for about 15–20 minutes or until a knife inserted in the middle comes out clean. Keep an eye to not overcook them. They won't brown much, so don't wait until they do! Set buns aside to cool. (You could prepare the burgers now, if you like.)

BURGER

NUTRITIONAL DATA PER BURGER
182kcals, 21g protein, 5g carbs, 4g fat, 1g fiber

INGREDIENTS
1 chopped onion
1 garlic clove
1 1/2 cups lean or extra-lean organic ground beef
1/4 cup rolled oats (gluten-free or regular)
1 egg
1 teaspoon paprika
1 tablespoon tomato puree or sundried tomato paste
1 teaspoon ground cumin
1 teaspoon pepper
Salt to taste
Toppings: ketchup, mayo, mustard, tomato, lettuce (or other greens), avocado, sliced sweet potato, cheese, etc.

DIRECTIONS
1. Over medium heat, preheat a nonstick pan, further nonsticked with some coconut oil or low-cal spray. Add the onion and sauté it until it's soft and caramelizes a bit. Put onions in a large bowl and wipe out pan.

2. Add all the above ingredients into a big bowl, including the onion you just fried up. Mix it all together using your hands and shape five patties (or six if you want to make them smaller!).

3. Heat the same pan, nonsticked again with coconut oil or spray. When pan is hot, lay the burgers in it. Then turn the heat down to medium so the bottom "seals up" nicely and the rest of the burger cooks.

4. Slice your buns in half, add your burger, some tomato, lettuce (or other greens), avocado, etc. You can add some sliced sweet potato even or a fried egg and of course ketchup and mayo +/- mustard! You can also throw on some blue cheese or goat's cheese or Gruyère or whatever you like best on your burgers!

WHO DOESN'T LOVE A BEEF BURGER, RIGHT? WELL... VEGANS. OK. LET ME REPHRASE.

Have you ever met a meat-eater who doesn't love a good beef burger? I haven't. Beef burgers are one of the best-liked foods out there!

They're great because you can fill them with pretty much whatever you like, you can stack them as high as you think your mouth can stretch (even though, often, it can't), and alongside a plate of (sweet potato) fries, well . . . they're fantastic. The problem with most burgers out there, though, is that they're not very healthy, high as they are in fats and quite often hydrogenated oils too. Then you look at the bun and your heart can break a little because there's nothing healthy about a regular burger bun—it's just carbs, in the form of simple sugars. Obviously it's fine to eat a regular burger every once in a while but frequently? I'm not too sure. That's why I created these healthy burgers! You can eat them weekly if you want. You can incorporate them into your healthy diet plan too, no problem. You can fill them with veggies, with bacon, with avocado—with pretty much anything you want! Check it out:

PROTEIN
QUICHE
SOUP &
OTHER SAVORY FOODS

I AM AT A FRENCH CAFÉ IN LONDON WITH A GROUP OF FRIENDS. THE PLACE WE'RE AT SERVES ONLY SANDWICHES, CROISSANTS, MUFFINS, AND QUICHE.

I'm hungry. I just finished a workout. I want to order something healthy, something containing protein and ideally some veggies. I consider buying a chicken sandwich and "gutting" it (removing its insides and leaving the bread shell behind), but I quickly realize there's only about a third of a chicken breast in each sandwich, and, considering its price tag, the whole thing would be a colossal waste of money. So, what do I do? I order a large chicken-and-vegetable quiche. I order it and eat it with gusto, scooping out the egg, chicken, and veggies, leaving the pastry behind. Why do I do this? I do it because I don't see pastry as a great addition to the system; you're better off not eating it. But let's be honest, a quiche without a crust is kind of like a bun-less burger: an impostor, a has-been, a once-was—a boo-hoo-hoo. Because the crust is meant to complement the filling, to offset the textures, to bring balance to the whole dish. That is why I made this recipe, so I never have to scoop the inside from a quiche again. :-)

SMOKED SALMON & ROSEMARY PROTEIN QUICHE TARTLETS

SERVINGS

2 quiche tartlets

NUTRITIONAL DATA PER SERVING

240kcals, 31.7g protein, 6.1g carbs, 8.2g fat, 3.8g fiber

INGREDIENTS

CRUST

2 egg whites

1/4 cup pea protein powder

2 tablespoons coconut flour

2 tablespoons milk

1 teaspoon dried rosemary

1 teaspoon onion granules

FILLING

2 eggs

1/4 cup smoked salmon, chopped

2 tablespoons almond milk

Salt and herbs

    (I use onion granules, garlic salt, pepper, and dried basil)

DIRECTIONS

1. Preheat oven to 375°F (around 190°C).

2. Blend the crust ingredients together (using an immersion blender, mixer, or food processor). You'll end up with a wet, doughy batter.

3. Scoop this batter with a spoon and press it into either a medium-size pie/quiche/tart tin or a few small ones. I ended up using two little ones to make individual quiches, but you can do it however you like, to cater to your own bakeware and so on.

4. Once your dough is pressed into the tins (you can use your fingers or a little spoon to press it in), bake for about 15 minutes, or until it starts to brown. When it does, take it out, allow it to cool, and top it with your quiche filling!

5. To make the filling, whisk the eggs with the smoked salmon, herbs, seasoning, and a couple of tablespoons of milk for two small quiche or tartlet crusts. Some people add cream to the egg mixture to make it smoother, so go ahead and add some if you want instead of milk. Consider also adding some chopped red peppers, onions, and broccoli! The sky's the limit to what you can fill your quiche with; there are so many killer combos!

6. Bake the crusts with the filling for another 30 minutes or until the egg has set nicely.

PROTEIN QUICHE LORRAINE

A quiche Lorraine is a quiche that's made with bacon, lardons, or pancetta. It's not called "Lorraine" because the person who invented it was called that. It's called "Lorraine" because it originates from the Lorraine region of France. There are dozens of different varieties of quiche Lorraine. Some exclude cheese, others include it; some use a bread-based crust, others go for puff pastry; some people include vegetables in the filling, and others stick to just bacon. You can find hundreds of different kinds of quiche Lorraine out there! But there's one kind you won't be able to find anywhere other than the confines of your own kitchen: a Protein Quiche Lorraine—a super healthy and absolutely finger-lickingly sublime Protein Quiche Lorraine. Welcome to this recipe! ;-)

SERVINGS
1 quiche

NUTRITIONAL DATA PER 1/8 QUICHE
113kcals, 8g protein, 5g carbs, 6g fat

1/4 cup brown rice flour
1/4 cup unflavored pea protein powder
1 egg
1/4 cup milk
1/2 teaspoon onion granules (optional but nice)

3–4 slices of bacon (depending on how "bacon-y" you want it)
1 onion, chopped
4 eggs
1/4 cup Swiss or Gruyère cheese
2 tablespoons cream

1. Preheat oven to 350°F (around 175°C).

2. Using a handheld blender or food processor, blend together all the crust ingredients until you get a sort of paste or dough.

3. Press the dough into a medium-size quiche springform pan, using a silicone spatula to make sure you cover the base of the pan and most of the sides.

4. Bake until crust has cooked through (around 10–12 minutes).

FILLING

1. First, fry your bacon. You can fry it in a nonstick pan, or, if you want it a bit lower in fat, just stick it under the broiler or oven grill (that way, a lot of the fat melts off).

2. Once your bacon is nice and crispy, chop it into strips, or, if you want to make it more traditionally French, into dice.

3. Meanwhile, fry your onion in a nonstick pan with some coconut oil or low-calorie spray. Fry it until it's brown and has caramelized slightly.

4. Whisk the eggs with the bacon and the rest of the ingredients and pour it into your cooked quiche crust.

5. Bake at 325°F (around 160°C) until the filling has cooked through (around 30–35 minutes).

PARMESAN & SUNDRIED TOMATO PROTEIN QUICHE TARTLETS

SERVINGS
2 quiche tartlets

NUTRITIONAL DATA PER SERVING
245kcals, 24.9g protein, 17.7g carbs, 8.25g fat, 2.2g fiber

INGREDIENTS

CRUST
1/4 cup + 1 tablespoon oat flour

3 tablespoons pea protein powder

1 egg

2 tablespoons almond milk

Salt and herbs (I use onion granules, garlic salt, pepper, and dried basil)

FILLING
1 egg

7 sundried tomatoes (in extra-virgin olive oil or plain)

1 tablespoon grated Parmesan cheese

2 tablespoons milk

Salt and herbs (again, I use onion granules, garlic salt, pepper, and dried basil)

DIRECTIONS

1. Preheat oven to 350°F (around 175°C).

2. First, make your crust by blending all the crust ingredients together, using a blender or mixer.

3. Then, press all the batter into two mini pie or quiche tins using a spoon (the batter will be mushy, not doughy, and that's fine; just press it down flat in your pie tin).

4. Bake the crusts for about 30 minutes, or until they're browned.

5. When they're done, remove them from the oven and make your filling. The filling is extremely easy: all you need to do is whisk all the filling ingredients together, and then pour the mixture into the crusts. Bake the crusts with the filling for another 30 minutes or until the egg has set nicely.

TARRAGON PROTEIN BLINI

These blini are low-carb and contain only four ingredients, one of them a spice: tarragon. Tarragon is somewhat of an "underdog" herb, isn't it? It's not as popular or well known as basil, rosemary, thyme, parsley, oregano, coriander, etc., but, oh, what an herb it is! Tarragon goes deliciously well with chicken, especially in white creamy sauces (mmmm), but it also goes really well with eggs (all hail eggs Benedictus) and fish (enter here, salmon—nommmmmm).

SERVINGS
8 small pancakes
NUTRITIONAL DATA
WITHOUT SALMON OR EXTRA
HUMMUS, BECAUSE YOU CAN,
AFTER ALL, FILL THEM WITH
WHATEVER YOU LIKE
235kcals, 34.5g protein, 5.5g carbs , 8.3g fat , 1g fiber

INGREDIENTS

BLINI
1/4 cup liquid egg whites
1/4 cup pea protein powder
1 tablespoon prepared hummus
1 teaspoon dried tarragon

TOPPINGS
Cheese, smoked salmon, hummus, avocado, pate, ham, etc.
 (Salmon is particularly nice.)

DIRECTIONS

1. Whisk all ingredients together.

2. Preheat nonstick pan, further nonsticked with some low-fat cooking spray or coconut oil.

3. Pour about eight small blobs of batter into the pan, as you would pancakes.

4. Flip when bubbles start appearing on their surface and remove from the pan when fully cooked.

5. Top with whatever you like.

Now, you may be thinking, "Come on, woman, those are mini pancakes! Why not just call them that?" Well, I find these guys fall more under the blini category than the mini pancake category. Why? Mostly because of their consistency, overall texture, and mild flavor.

A THREE-MINUTE EGG & SOME SWEET POTATO PROTEIN SOLDIERS

Before I moved to England, I had no idea what Eggs and Soldiers was.

I remember the first time I encountered this dish. I was sitting in a restaurant, going over the breakfast menu, and there, between omelets and fried eggs, it said "Eggs and Soldiers." I looked up and asked my (American) friend, "What is THAT?" but she shrugged and told me that she had "absolutely no idea." So we both ordered it (my friends and I are wiiiild like that).

I honestly didn't know what to expect. I thought it had to be something containing egg, but the "soldiers" bit threw me off. Then the waiter came, and I saw it. It was basically just a boiled egg and sliced pieces of toast! I found it a bit . . . anticlimactic. I don't know. I expected something more . . . combative. Something more . . . epic? But instead I got toast. Plain old-fashioned . . . toast.

When I got home, I did some research and found out that these thinly sliced pieces of toast are called "soldiers" because they're evocative of soldiers on parade. Now, how this is the case, I just don't know. Apparently, it's because they're sliced up to stand tall and straight and then laid out on the plate as if they're standing at attention. I personally think this is all very humorous. I mean, who came up with this?! And under what circumstances?! It's very strange. But kind of funny at the same time, don't you think?

Anyway, in a spirit of British communitas, let me introduce you to THESE handsome protein soldiers! They're gorgeous. Seriously. They're one of the tastiest soldiers I've ever dipped into yolk and far superior to any kind of toast I've ever had. They owe their tastiness to the sweet potato flour, which adds this subtle sweetness that goes magically well with the pea protein powder. I'm quite impressed by this whole thing, to be honest, because it was an experiment—it was my first time cooking with sweet potato flour. And I'm impressed. Seriously impressed.

SERVINGS
2 battalions

NUTRITIONAL DATA PER SERVING
188.2kcals, 27.3g protein, 15.1g carbs, 1.9g fat

INGREDIENTS
1/4 cup unflavored pea protein powder
1/4 cup sweet potato flour
3/4 cup liquid egg whites
1 egg

DIRECTIONS

1. Preheat a nonstick frying pan, further nonsticked with some low-calorie cooking spray or coconut oil. Turn the heat to high.

2. Mix all the ingredients except the egg, and spread the batter into the pan like a big fat pancake (it'll be chunky and thick; just press it down with a spatula). When you do this, turn the heat down to medium.

3. While that is cooking, prepare a soft-boiled egg: Bring a small pan of water to a boil, carefully drop in your egg (shell and all). Cover pan, turn off heat, and wait 5 minutes. Remove egg from pan, rinse in cold water, and prop in egg dish or bowl.

4. Once your "pancake" has cooked, flip it, slice it into strips, and BOOM! You got yourself some soldiers. :-D

5. Tap the top of the eggshell and peel enough so that you can eat it with your soldiers.

IT'S A RECURRING SCENE AT COCKTAIL PARTIES, WEDDINGS, CONFERENCE DINNERS, ETC.

There I am, holding a glass of whatever (usually a wine I'm trying to convince myself I actually quite like or a bit of champagne I'm trying to successfully sip through). Small talk, blah blah blah, more small talk, blah, and then, suddenly, BOOM! There it is: the tray of hors d'oeuvres making its way around the room. Oh! Joy of joys! This is the tricky part: looking unmoved— appearing calm, cool, and collected. See, my view is that one shouldn't look too excited about the hors d'oeuvres. One should remain casual, try to really focus on the conversation, and then slowly and inconspicuously push all parties closer and closer to the man (or woman) with the Tray. I just think, what's not to love about them? Creativity blossoms in the land of the hors d'oeuvre—anything goes. This is why, sometimes, I love to have a meal made up of just a bunch of hors d'oeuvres—just like these!

PUMPKIN PROTEIN BLINI

SERVINGS

8 blini

NUTRITIONAL DATA FOR ALL 8 BLINI

229kcals, 34g protein, 17g carbs, 3.4g fat, 13.5g fiber

INGREDIENTS

1/2 cup liquid egg whites

1 tablespoon coconut flour

1 tablespoon flaxseeds or psyllium husks

1 tablespoon pumpkin puree

2 tablespoons pea protein powder

DIRECTIONS

1. Whisk all ingredients together.

2. Preheat nonstick pan, further nonsticked with some low-fat cooking spray or coconut oil.

3. Pour about eight small blobs of batter into the pan, as you would for pancakes.

4. Flip when bubbles start appearing on their surface and remove from the pan when fully cooked.

PUMPKIN MACARONI & CHEESE

The purists among you will probably violently recoil after reading what's in my mac and cheese: pumpkin. Yes, pumpkin. And coconut. And pea protein powder. It sounds strange, I know, but it works! Check it out.

SERVINGS
4 small bowls

NUTRITIONAL DATA PER SERVING
163kcals, 10.1g protein, 15.2g carbs, 6g fat, 3.15g fiber

INGREDIENTS
1 cup brown rice macaroni

2 tablespoons coconut flour

1 cup milk

2 tablespoons pea protein powder

1/2 teaspoon cheddar powder

2 tablespoons pumpkin puree

1/2 teaspoon sea salt

1/2 teaspoon onion granules

1/4 cup grated cheddar cheese (plus extra for topping)

DIRECTIONS

1. Cook pasta according to directions on the box, and drain.

2. Meanwhile, in a saucepan, mix together the rest of the ingredients to make a sauce.

3. Gently stir cooked pasta into sauce and divide the macaroni into four little ramekins or mini-casserole-pot-thingies.

4. Add a bit more grated cheese on top of each mini-casserole. This is optional, but it adds a really nice cheesy crust to the pasta dish!

MAC N CHEESE

This Mac N Cheese recipe, unlike the one before it, yields a more "authentic"-tasting Mac N Cheese. That's not to say that this recipe is better than the one before it; it's just different. Try both and see which one you like best! Or play around with either recipe to create a third recipe of your own, custom-made to fit the desires and demands of your unique set of taste buds. ;-)

SERVINGS
2 bowls
NUTRITIONAL DATA PER BOWL
281kcals, 26g protein, 27g carbs, 8g fat, 1g fiber

INGREDIENTS

1/2 cup rice macaroni

1/4 cup unflavored pea protein powder

3/4 cup milk

1/4 cup grated cheese (plus additional cheese for topping)

1–2 tablespoons cheddar powder (depending on how cheesy you
    like your mac n cheese!)

DIRECTIONS

1. Cook the macaroni according to the instructions on the box. Drain.

2. Meanwhile, in a saucepan, whisk the rest of the ingredients together over medium heat.

3. Once a sauce has formed, mix it in with the macaroni. At this stage you can either eat it like it is or stick it under the broiler with some extra cheese on top—if you want a cheesy layer on top!

PROTEIN TORTILLA CHIPS WITH SALSA & NACHO STUFF

SERVINGS
2 servings of 8 chips each

NUTRITIONAL DATA PER SERVING
168kcals, 18.75g protein, 11.9g carbs, 5.3g fat , 4.5g fiber

I always like having protein snacks around when people come over; you know, to protect my reputation and so on, hee hee. ;-) I made these for a Super Bowl party because they're just so versatile! And yummy! And open to being eaten in lots of different ways. I like to serve these with salsa and "nacho stuff" (beef, avocado, more salsa, cheese, etc.) on top, but they're also great to dip into cream cheese, salmon mousse, or hummus!

Double or triple the recipe to make more, and remember: if they lose their crunch, stick them back under the broiler. That'll crunch them back up.

INGREDIENTS

1 large egg white
1/4 cup unflavored whey protein powder
1/4 cup oat flour
2 tablespoons flaxseeds
Sea salt to taste
Paprika to taste
Cumin to taste

DIRECTIONS

1. First, blend the above ingredients and fry up the batter on a hot, hot, hot pan to create one giant pancake.

2. Spread the batter as thin as possible and remember to coat your pan with coconut oil, low-cal cooking spray, or butter, so it definitely won't stick.

3. Once bubbles start appearing on the pancake's surface, flip it. Then remove it from the pan, cut it into triangles, then cut each triangle in half, and stick them under the broiler until they are brown and crisp.

4. Then flip them so the other side crunches up nicely, too.

CHUNKY CREAM OF ONION, GARLIC & PEA PROTEIN SOUP

Before I took up weightlifting and decided to stop running as my primary form of exercise, I used to get sick a lot. Breathe Easy, Throat Coat, and Cold Season were always in my tea cabinet. I'm not talking about anything serious. I'd just attract everyone else's common cold and, four to five times a year, I'd find myself zombieing around the house with a rapidly shrinking box of tissues. Nowadays, I hardly ever get sick. I say "hardly ever" and not "never," because, well, I had a cold when I first made this recipe. That's right, for the second time in three years, I sounded like Donald Duck.

I wanted to make myself a vegetable-and-chicken soup to begin with but then realized that there wasn't any chicken in the fridge, and I looked too much like Death to venture into the world of the living and get some. That's when creativity knocked, and in came this recipe! Even in my state of languor, I was buzzing with excitement as I ate this :-)

SERVINGS
1 bowl
NUTRITIONAL DATA PER SERVING WITHOUT OLIVE OIL
281kcals, 30g protein, 37.1g carbs, 2.5g fat

INGREDIENTS

1 large onion, roughly chopped

1 large carrot, peeled and roughly chopped

2 garlic cloves

1/4 cup unflavored pea protein powder

1/4 cup coconut milk

1 tablespoon extra-virgin olive oil

Fresh basil, for garnish

Dash of cayenne pepper (optional)

DIRECTIONS

1. Steam the vegetables over boiling water until they're soft, or sauté them in a large soup pot.

2. Then, using an immersion blender or potato masher, mash the vegetables with the pea protein powder and milk. Keep on going for a creamier texture, but I quite like the chunky texture.

3. To top it all off, add the olive oil (which not only tastes smashing but is a great way to ensure that the fat-soluble vitamins from the vegetables are well absorbed by the system), some fresh basil, and BOOOM! Red chili powder! This is optional but, to me, absolutely delicious!

BROCCOLI & CHEESE PROTEIN SOUP

This is one of my favorite recipes to make when it's really cold out and I want something that's warming, tasty, and nutritious. Making this soup is very easy and takes no time at all. Sometimes I eat it on its own, sometimes I add a bit of cream on top, and sometimes I even eat it inside a scooped-out protein bread roll! So consider doing that too. You could even add some crispy bacon, protein croutons, or pieces of chicken!

SERVINGS

2–3 bowls

NUTRITIONAL DATA PER SERVING

226kcals, 20g protein, 14g carbs, 8g fat, 4g fiber

INGREDIENTS

1 teaspoon butter or coconut oil

1 small onion, chopped

1 garlic clove, chopped

1 head of broccoli, steamed and chopped
   (approximately 1 cup)

1 1/4 cups milk (almond or cow's will do)

1/4 cup pea protein powder

2 tablespoons grated cheddar

1/2 teaspoon chicken stock

1 tablespoon cream (optional but lovely!)

DIRECTIONS

1. Heat butter or coconut oil in a large soup pot.

2. Add the onion and garlic and stir well; then cover the pot. Let things cook for 10–15 minutes, or until onion is transparent and soft.

3. Add the steamed broccoli and, using an immersion blender, liquefy the broccoli with the rest of the ingredients. You can also let the mixture cool and blend it in a regular blender, then reheat it before serving.

4. Add a dollop of cream to the soup when serving—this is optional but really tasty!

SWEET POTATO PROTEIN SOUP

Potatoes lend a great texture and a wonderful creaminess to soup. That's why so many traditional soup recipes include them. Usually though, potato-containing soups are made with white as opposed to sweet potatoes. This has a lot to do with their flavor—white potatoes are milder and, as a result, easier to feature in the background as opposed to the forefront of a soup. What if we want to use the potato as the primary ingredient for our soup? Then I think the sweet potato wins. It's sweeter, more flavorsome, and if you combine it with caramelized onions, some garlic, almond milk, and pea protein? Well, well, well. You've got yourself a winner. :-)

SERVINGS
2 bowls

NUTRITIONAL DATA PER SERVING
176kcals, 8g protein, 22g carbs , 7g fat, 4g fiber

INGREDIENTS
1 teaspoon coconut oil or butter

1 small red onion, chopped

1 garlic clove, chopped

1 large cooked sweet potato
    (boiled, baked, or roasted until soft)

2 cups coconut or almond milk

2 tablespoons unflavored pea protein powder

1 teaspoon nutmeg (optional but nice)

1 teaspoon salt

DIRECTIONS
1. Heat the butter or coconut oil in a large soup pot on high heat.

2. Add the onion and garlic, stir them around, and turn your heat down to medium. Cover the pot and let things cook for 5–10 minutes, or until the onion is soft and slightly caramelized.

3. Add the cooked sweet potato, milk, protein powder, and seasonings.

4. Then, using an immersion blender, liquefy the vegetables with the rest of the ingredients. You can also let the mixture cool and blend it in a regular blender, then reheat it before serving.

5. If soup is too thick, add a little milk until it has the consistency you like!

PROTEIN
BARS
CHOCOLATES

A NOTE ON MELTING CHOCOLATE

Many of the bars and chocolate truffles in this chapter and the next are dipped in chocolate. I like to use dark chocolate bars with between 75 and 100 percent cocoa. The percentage refers to how much of the chocolate bar is actually made from the cocoa bean. The remainder is usually sugar, vanilla, and sometimes an emulsifier. Cocoa has fiber in it, too, so the more cocoa, the better. Also, the darker your bar (i.e., the higher its cocoa percentage), the richer in antioxidants it will be! So try to use dark chocolate when you follow my recipes. Of course, if you want something sweeter, use a bar with a lower percentage of cocoa.

Always break the chocolate into small pieces for even melting. I always melt it in a bain marie—a glass bowl on top of a pot of simmering water. This ensures the chocolate melts evenly and doesn't burn. You can stir it gently as it melts, but don't let any water or moisture get into the chocolate, or it will clump up and turn weird on you.

DIPPING OR COATING BARS WITH CHOCOLATE

Once you have your bowl of melted chocolate, you can drop one bar at a time into it using your hands. You can use a spatula to do this, too, but if your bars or truffles are soft, using a spatula might break them. If you don't want to use your hand, what I suggest you do is just place the bars on a tray lined with aluminum foil and pour the melted chocolate on top to cover the other side in chocolate, too.

PROTEIN MAGIC BARS

SERVINGS
5 bars

NUTRITIONAL DATA PER SERVING
207.84kcals, 24.2g protein, 14.16g carbs, 4.9g fat, 3.84g fiber

I'm a HUGE fan of homemade protein bars. You know why? Because they're eons ahead of store-bought protein bars. They're so much healthier! Even the really "clean" protein bars out there all contain a bunch of questionable ingredients—stuff like sugar, hydrogenated fats, sketchy sweeteners, and inferior sources of protein. This is why I'm such a strong proponent of people making their own protein bars at home: you can design them to deliver not just protein and fiber but also antioxidants, healthy fats, and lots of vitamins and minerals. And you can completely eliminate any and all dubious ingredients.

INGREDIENTS

BASE
3/4 cup liquid egg whites
1/2 cup goji berries
1/2 cup vanilla pea protein powder
1/2 cup milk (almond or coconut)
3 tablespoons coconut flour

TOP
1/4 cup milk (almond or coconut)
1/4 cup cocoa powder
2 tablespoons date syrup
1/4 cup chocolate pea protein powder

DIRECTIONS

1. Preheat oven to 325˚F (around 160˚C).

2. Blend all the ingredients for the base together until you form a batter (let's call this the "base batter").

3. In a separate bowl, blend all the ingredients for the top (to form the "top batter").

4. Flatten the base batter in a small brownie pan (ideally silicone), and then flatten the top batter on top. Use a knife, spatula, or plain old spoon for this.

5. Bake it for about 35–40 minutes, or until a knife inserted into the middle comes out clean.

6. Slice the whole thing into bars and MUUUUUUNCH!!!!!

THE INCREDIBLE BANANA-NUT PROTEIN BARS

Banana and nut—it's a timeless combination, kind of like apple and vanilla, cherry and chocolate, lemon and poppy seeds, cinnamon and orange, and jelly and peanut butter! You just can't argue against these remarkable pairings! The combination of banana and nut in particular is great! It yields delicious muffins, cakes, breads, and as you're about to find out . . . protein bars. ;-)

These bars are awesome to carry with you to school, to work, or on a trip! They last a couple of days unrefrigerated, and oy they're delicious! Gorgeously nutty and perfectly balanced, and texture-wise not too dry or at all mushy. Everyone who tries them is totally shocked that these are protein bars, not cookie bars. BAAAAM! Turning protein skeptics into protein lovers, one bite POW at a time. ;-)

SERVINGS
5 bars

NUTRITIONAL DATA PER SERVING
181kcals, 11g protein, 12.7g carbs, 8.9g fat, 4.8g fiber

INGREDIENTS
1 small banana

1/2 cup rolled oats (gluten-free or regular)

1/4 cup chopped almonds

4 Brazil nuts, chopped

2 tablespoons coconut flour

6 tablespoons unflavored whey protein powder

6 tablespoons milk (I use hemp milk, but any will do)

1 teaspoon chicory powder (optional)

DIRECTIONS
1. Preheat oven to 325°F (around 160°C).

2. Blend together all the ingredients with an immersion blender, blender, or food processor until smooth.

3. Spread the batter in a small pan (a loaf pan will do).

4. Bake for about 35 minutes, or until a knife inserted in the middle comes out clean.

THE BEST PROTEIN BROWNIE BARS IN THE WORLD

These protein brownie bars are great. They're impeccably balanced in flavor, extremely chocolatey, and mm-mm-mmmmmm! They're just faultless. Brownie bars are a perfect snack for school and work. Just wrap them in aluminum foil, and BOOOOOOM—you're ready to go!

SERVINGS

5 bars

NUTRITIONAL DATA PER SERVING

146.14kcals, 16.2g protein, 10.9g carbs, 3.58g fat, 3.2g fiber

INGREDIENTS

3/4 cup almond milk

1/2 cup prunes (if you hate prunes, use medjool dates, instead)

1/2 cup pea protein powder, brown rice protein powder, or other veggie protein blend

1/4 cup cocoa powder

1/4 cup coconut flour

1/2 cup liquid egg whites

3/4 teaspoon baking soda

DIRECTIONS

1. Preheat oven to 325°F (around 160°C).

2. Using an immersion blender, blender, or food processor, blend all the ingredients together.

3. Bake your batter in a small silicone brownie pan until a knife inserted into the middle comes out clean (mine were done after about 38 minutes, but check on them after 30).

If you want to take it all up a notch, add some chopped nuts and/or some (dark) chocolate chips to the batter before baking. Pecans, walnuts, and macadamia nuts would be amazing! But the bars don't really need extra stuff; they're perfect as they are. :-) Another thing you can do is slice them up into squares instead of bars and call them brownies. Same thing, really. ;-)

THE BEST "RAW" WHEY PROTEIN BARS IN THE GALAXY

"Look at her. That woman with the sweatpants and the funny-looking-pig shirt, singing her lungs out like a buffoon. It looks like she's shaping some kind of dough into bars. Let's just hope that dough doesn't contain raw eggs, because if it does, this scene might turn into a Salmonella tragedy. She's smiling ear to ear and nomming like a lunatic. What's IN that dough!? She walks over to the counter, positions what are now bars on a plate, and grabs her camera. Snap. Snap. Snap. Snap . . . She's taking, like, a thousand pictures! And now . . . Holy Mongoose! She's devouring the bars!!! I've never seen someone savor a bar so intensely. The woman's on the verge of rapture here! Let's feel her heartbeat. Yes, it's elevated. All you can hear in this house is, 'MMM!!!!!!!!!!!!!!' The woman is delirious. What's going on!? Seriously, what's IN these bars!?"

SERVINGS

2 bars

NUTRITIONAL DATA PER SERVING

200kcals, 10g protein, 14g carbs , 12g fat, 5g fiber

INGREDIENTS

1 tablespoon coconut oil

2 tablespoons cocoa powder

1/4 cup unflavored whey protein powder

1 tablespoon coconut flour

2 tablespoons goji berries

2 tablespoons almond milk (or coconut, hemp, or rice milk)

1 tablespoon toffee flavoring drops or your sweetener of choice

2 tablespoons chopped hazelnuts

DIRECTIONS

1. Using a blender or food processor, mix the above ingredients until you get a paste.

2. Taste this paste to ensure it's sweet enough for you. If it isn't, add more sweetener (e.g., toffee flavoring drops or stevia drops or honey or date syrup!).

3. Shape this paste into bars (or you could shape it into truffles).

4. Put in the fridge for an hour.

5. Eat.

STRAWBERRY & DARK CHOCOLATE PROTEIN BARS

I've tried dozens, if not hundreds, of protein bars in the US, the UK, and elsewhere in Europe. You name the bar, and I've probably had it. And none of them compare—none of them even come CLOSE—to homemade protein bars. It's crazy. It's like comparing apples to . . . play dough. Homemade protein bars should be in everyone's repertoire of recipes.

SERVINGS
3 bars
NUTRITIONAL DATA PER SERVING
210kcals, 18g protein, 10g carbs, 9g fat, 6g fiber

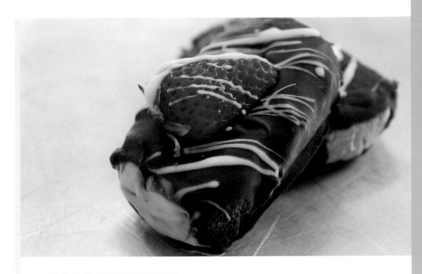

INGREDIENTS

1/2 cup strawberry whey protein powder
6 tablespoons coconut flour
6 tablespoons almond milk
1/2 bar (50g) dark chocolate
2 tablespoons chopped strawberries
1/10 bar (10g) white chocolate

DIRECTIONS

1. Mix together the protein powder, coconut flour, and almond milk. Shape the batter into three bars, and place on a cookie sheet lined with parchment paper or wax paper. For best results, chill bars for 20–30 minutes in the refrigerator (this is optional, but it makes the coating easier).

2. Meanwhile, melt your dark chocolate as described on page 141.

3. Dip or coat bars in chocolate and return them to the parchment-lined cookie sheet. You can add a chopped strawberry on top as I did, along with some extra melted chocolate. I melted the white chocolate and just poured that on top for aesthetics, but that is optional. :-)

4. Place in freezer or refrigerator until chocolate has hardened, and voilà! DONE! Protein bar deliciousness.

BLUEBERRY & VANILLA PROTEIN BARS

I made these bars to munch on our way to the Rocky Mountains. I didn't blend the blueberries into the bars because I thought keeping them whole would be more fun, and indeed it was. ;-) We ended up munching these bars on our way from New Mexico to Colorado, and did we enjoy them! The blueberries burst with every bite, and nom, nom, nommmm, I highly recommend you try them. :-)))))

SERVINGS
8 small bars
NUTRITIONAL DATA PER SERVING
59kcals, 4g protein, 3g carbs, 3g fat

INGREDIENTS

1/4 cup vanilla whey protein powder
2 tablespoons coconut flour
1/4 cup almond milk
1/2 cup blueberries (fresh, but freeze-dried would be really nice, too)
1/3 bar (30g) dark chocolate

LOVE ALWAYS FINDS A WHEY

DIRECTIONS

1. In a bowl, mix all the above ingredients except for the blueberries and chocolate. Add more coconut flour if the mixture seems too wet, or more milk if it seems too dry.

2. Add the blueberries to the mix and shape the batter into eight small bars; place on a cookie sheet lined with parchment paper or wax paper. For best results, chill bars for 20–30 minutes in the refrigerator (optional).

3. Meanwhile, melt chocolate as described on page 141. Dip or coat bars in chocolate and return them to the parchment-lined cookie sheet. Place in the freezer or refrigerator until chocolate has hardened.

CARNIVOROUS PROTEIN BARS

Vegans and vegetarians, be warned. This post contains beef protein powder. Have you tried it? I bet that, mobilizing the formula "chocolate/vanilla + beef = nasty," you're probably thinking that it must not taste so great, to put it mildly. You're wrong, though. It actually tastes good—damn good. :-D Does it taste like beef? Well, yes and no. Yes, because it definitely has beefy undertones (imagine super ground-up beef jerky?), but no, because it then has a gorgeous sweetness that takes over the beef! The bars are really mild and actually caramel-y, a flavor that goes deliciously well alongside the hints of orange I mix in there. Overall, it's an interesting bar, and I actually doubt that, if we had a protein bar tasting, anyone would conclude this these bars contain beef!

INGREDIENTS

1/4 cup chocolate beef protein powder

3 tablespoons coconut flour

2 tablespoons chocolate pea protein powder

3/4 cup coconut milk

1 teaspoon grated orange peel

1/3 bar (30g) dark chocolate

DIRECTIONS

1. Mix together all the ingredients except for the chocolate. Shape the batter into four bars, and place on a cookie sheet lined with parchment paper or wax paper. For best results, chill bars for 20–30 minutes in the refrigerator (optional).

2. Meanwhile, melt chocolate as described on page 141. Dip or coat bars in chocolate and return them to the parchment-lined cookie sheet. Place in the freezer or refrigerator until chocolate has hardened. BOOM! Ready. :-D

SERVINGS

4 bars

NUTRITIONAL DATA PER SERVING

166.5kcals, 16.1g protein, 6.2g carbs, 6.4g fat, 5.4g fiber

I WARN YOU: IF YOU LIKE TIRAMISU AND YOU'RE INTO PROTEIN, YOU'RE GOING TO LOVE THESE BARS!

TIRAMISU PROTEIN BARS

SERVINGS

9 bars

NUTRITIONAL DATA PER SERVING

150kcals, 11g protein, 9g carbs, 8g fat, 5g fiber

INGREDIENTS

CAKEY BIT

1/2 cup liquid egg whites

1/4 cup chocolate or mocha cappuccino–
    flavored whey protein powder

1 tablespoon cocoa powder

1/4 cup rolled oats (gluten-free or regular)

1 tablespoon coconut flour

1 teaspoon instant coffee powder

2 tablespoons Greek yogurt

1 tablespoon Tia Maria (optional but nice)

FILLING

3 heaping tablespoons low-fat cream cheese
    or mascarpone

2 tablespoons vanilla whey protein powder

TOPPING

1 bar (100g) 85 percent dark chocolate

DIRECTIONS

1. Preheat oven to 350˚F (around 175˚C).

2. Blend together all the cakey bit ingredients and spread into a small brownie pan.

3. Bake for about 20 minutes, or until a knife inserted into the middle comes out clean. Make sure you don't overbake here, because if you do, they'll turn out pretty dry, and we don't want that. :-)

4. Meanwhile, prepare the filling by mixing together the cream cheese and protein powder. Begin melting the chocolate as described on page 141.

5. Let the cake layer cool before you cut it into bars, and then horizontally slice each bar in half. Stuff them with your cream cheese filling (spread filling on one half and top with the other half).

6. Carefully dip or coat bars in chocolate and place them on a parchment-lined cookie sheet. Chill in the freezer for 40 minutes and . . . nommage!

I'M A LITTLE CRAZY . . . CRAZY ABOUT (DELICIOUS AND HEALTHY) FOOD! AND IT'S A FAMILY THING, THIS LOVE OF ALL THINGS COOKING.

What makes it fun in our case is that we're equally passionate about exercise and nutrition. It was my dad, in fact, who got me hooked on strength training, and we always accompany our food chat with updates on our most recent exercise routines and accomplishments ("Dad! I got a deadlift PR!" or "Yesterday I rowed another marathon!" or "I was doing pull-ups at home, and the bar fell out with me on it, ha-ha-ha!"). We also talk a hell of a lot about fast- and short-twitch muscle fibers. It's my dad's favorite topic, for some reason.

Why am I telling you all this? I'm telling you so you understand why my recipes are jam-packed with exclamation marks and overexcitement! It's not that I exaggerate or am a ridiculously over-the-top person, it's because when I experiment with my protein and it ends up working out, I just want to shouuuuut and share it with the world! And my recipes end up receiving hyperbolic titles, and an inordinate amount of exclamation marks. But bear with me, okay?

Take, for example, these bars. They're gluten-free; high in antioxidants, magnesium, iron, essential fats, vitamin A, and calcium; and devoid of natural flavorings, fillers, preservatives, stabilizers, AND artificial sweeteners! They're also ridiculously tasty. What's not to love?!

BACON & CHILI DARK CHOCOLATE PROTEIN BARS

SERVINGS

5 small bars

NUTRITIONAL DATA PER SERVING

206kcals, 13g protein, 12g carbs, 11g fat

INGREDIENTS

1/2 cup chocolate whey protein powder

1/4 cup coconut flour

1/4 cup cacao nibs

2 tablespoons xylitol (or granulated stevia)

1/2 cup coconut milk (or almond or rice milk)

1/4 teaspoon cayenne pepper

2 strips (20g) cooked bacon, crumbled

1/2 bar (50g) 85 percent dark chocolate

DIRECTIONS

1. Blend together all ingredients except for the bacon and chocolate until you get a sort of dough. Then fold in the bacon.

2. The mixture should be firm enough to shape into bars. If it's too watery or sticky, add more coconut flour or protein powder. If it's too dry, add a bit more liquid.

3. Shape the batter into five small bars, and place on a cookie sheet lined with parchment paper or wax paper. For best results, chill bars for 20–30 minutes in the refrigerator (optional).

4. Meanwhile, melt chocolate as described on page 141. Dip or coat bars in chocolate and return them to the parchment-lined cookie sheet. Place in the freezer or refrigerator until chocolate has hardened.

5. Store chilled.

PUMPKIN PIE PROTEIN BARS

Let me tell you about these bars: I made them using sugar-free white chocolate. Traditional white chocolate is predominantly cocoa butter and sugar. Does it have anything going for it, nutrition-wise? Well . . . it's basically 100 percent fat, 60 percent of it saturated. It doesn't feature any carbs or protein. It does, however, feature cocoa mass polyphenols, antioxidants, and some vitamin K and E. Is the stuff GREAT to munch on a daily basis? Errr . . . probably not. How about once a week? Hmm . . . depends how much we're talking about. ;-) I personally wouldn't make it a regular thing, because I think there are far more nutritious fats out there, and I'm too big a fan of dark chocolate to turn myself into a traitor. But every once in a while, if you love the flavor of white chocolate, why not get a bar of the (sugar-free) stuff? Just adapt the rest of your diet to fit a bit of cocoa fat into it. ;-)

SERVINGS

4 bars

NUTRITIONAL DATA PER SERVING

227kcals, 15.7g protein, 8g carbs, 10g fat, 6.2g fiber

INGREDIENTS

1/2 cup pumpkin pie whey and casein
protein powder blend

1/4 cup coconut flour

1/4 cup pumpkin puree

1/2 cup almond milk

1 bar (100g) sugar-free white chocolate

DIRECTIONS

1. In a big bowl, mix together the protein powder, coconut flour, pumpkin puree, and almond milk. Shape the mixture into four bars and place on a cookie sheet lined with parchment paper or wax paper.

2. Meanwhile, melt the white chocolate as described on page 141. You'll want to brush the melted chocolate onto the bars, since white chocolate melts a lot thicker—and stickier—than dark chocolate.

3. Once all the bars are coated, return them to the parchment-lined cookie sheet and transfer them to the fridge for an hour to allow the chocolate to set. That's it: you're done. :-)

THE GREAT DARK CHOCOLATE–COVERED PUMPKIN PROTEIN BAR

SERVINGS

4 bars

NUTRITIONAL DATA PER SERVING

174kcals, 10.5g protein, 6g carbs, 12g fat, 3.6g fiber

INGREDIENTS

1/2 cup pumpkin puree

6 tablespoons vanilla whey protein powder

1/2 cup ground almonds

2 tablespoons coconut flour

1/4 cup dried coconut (optional but nice;
    you could also use nuts!)

1/2 bar (50g) 85 percent chocolate

DIRECTIONS

1. Using a mixer or some vigorous fork action, blend together the pumpkin, protein powder, almonds, and coconut flour, adding water a tablespoon at a time until a pasty batter or dough has formed.

2. Once the mixture looks pasty and dry enough to bite into, divide it into quarters and form the mixture into bars (at this stage, you could coat them with the dried coconut or nuts).

3. Place bars on a cookie sheet lined with parchment paper or wax paper. For best results, chill bars for 20–30 minutes in the refrigerator (optional).

4. Meanwhile, melt chocolate as described on page 141. Dip or coat bars in chocolate and return them to the parchment-lined cookie sheet. Place in the freezer or refrigerator until chocolate has hardened.

5. Store chilled.

SWEET POTATO PROTEIN BARS

I don't know if you've noticed, but the fitness and nutrition world is OBSESSED with sweet potatoes. You know why? Because not only are sweet potatoes delicious, they're also a nutritional powerhouse. Did you know, for example, that an average-size sweet potato has over 700 percent of an adult's recommended daily value of vitamin A?! And 65 percent of vitamin C? 12 percent riboflavin and 26 percent vitamin B6? 15 percent niacin? 14 percent magnesium? 27 percent potassium?! The verdict is in: sweet potatoes are a superfood. That's why we all love them so much. :-) That's why I make sweet potato fries, sweet potato pizza crusts, sweet potato protein pies, sweet potato protein cakes, sweet potato protein pancakes, and now . . . sweet potato protein bars!

SERVINGS

4 small bars

NUTRITIONAL DATA PER SERVING

191.72kcals, 16.2g protein, 15.5g carbs, 3.2g fiber, 7g fat

INGREDIENTS

1 large cooked sweet potato (boiled or roasted), unsalted

1/2 cup vanilla pea protein powder (or rice protein powder or casein protein powder)

1 tablespoon date syrup (or agave syrup or honey)

1 tablespoon coconut flour

1 tablespoon flaxseeds

2 tablespoons milk

1/2 bar (50g) 90 percent dark chocolate

DIRECTIONS

1. Blend all the above ingredients together (except for the chocolate), shape the batter into four little bars, and place on a cookie sheet lined with parchment paper or wax paper. For best results, chill bars for 20–30 minutes in the refrigerator (optional).

2. Meanwhile, melt chocolate as described on page 141. Dip or coat bars in chocolate and return them to the parchment-lined cookie sheet. Place in the freezer or refrigerator until chocolate has hardened.

3. Store chilled. Voilà! Sweet Potato Protein Bars!

COFFEE & COCOA PROTEIN BREAKFAST BARS

I made these bars to eat on a flight from England to Sweden. They're low-carb, gluten-free, and dairy-free. I chose these because I knew I'd want something to keep me awake while I waited for my plane to board. My plan was to get a big cup of coffee, dunk these in there, and nom, nom, nom: jolt the system back to living the good life. ;-)

SERVINGS

6 bars

NUTRITIONAL DATA PER SERVING

128.82kcals, 13.1g protein, 5.9g carbs, 6g fat, 5g fiber

INGREDIENTS

1/4 cup chocolate pea or brown rice protein powder

1 cup liquid egg whites

1/2 cup cacao nibs

1/4 cup coconut flour

2 tablespoons stevia

1 tablespoon coffee

1/4 cup almond milk

DIRECTIONS

1. Preheat oven to 350°F (around 175°C).

2. Using an immersion blender, blender, or food processor, blend all ingredients together.

3. Bake for 20–30 minutes, or until they feel firm.

CRUNCHY CARAMEL & DARK CHOCOLATE PROTEIN BARS

You'll want to eat all of these bars when you make them, so make sure that someone's around to share them with you! Otherwise the spirit of greediness will engulf you and there'll be none left for anyone else. They're that good. But don't take my word for it, please. Make them. But consider yourself warned. ;-)

SERVINGS

4 bars

NUTRITIONAL DATA PER SERVING

275kcals, 15g protein, 26g carbs, 13g fat

INGREDIENTS

1/2 cup chocolate protein powder

1/4 cup coconut flour

1/4 cup ground almonds

1/2 cup almond milk (or your milk choice)

1/2 teaspoon caramel flavoring

6 large medjool dates, pitted

2 tablespoons ground nuts

About 1/2 bar (40g) dark chocolate

DIRECTIONS

1. Blend together the protein powder, coconut flour, almonds, milk, and flavoring until you get a dough that you can shape with your hands. If your mix is too wet, add a bit more coconut flour. If it's too dry, add a bit more milk.

2. Shape the batter into bars or truffles, whatever size you like. I made four bars. Place on a cookie sheet lined with parchment paper or wax paper.

3. Process the dates in a blender or food processor, or chop them finely by hand, until they have the consistency of caramel.

4. Spread a layer of date caramel on each bar, and sprinkle with chopped nuts, gently pushing them in to stick. For best results, chill bars for 20–30 minutes in the refrigerator (this is optional, but it makes the coating easier).

5. Meanwhile, melt your chocolate as described on page 141 and dip or coat bars with it.

6. Place in freezer or refrigerator until chocolate has hardened, and… BOOM! Done.

SCENE: SMALL KITCHEN. PROTEIN POWDER TUBS ON THE COUNTER.

A shopping bag with two lemons and a carton of eggs, and a woman wearing a Protein Pow apron while mixing a batter and singing "Africa" by Toto. The woman walks toward the shopping bag, takes out the lemons, grates and squeezes one of them into her batter, and then presses this batter inside a cake pan. She puts the pan in the oven.

"That's the crust, done," she says to herself.

She takes out another bowl, adds several ingredients to it, and makes another mix. She adds some lemon juice to it, too. After about fifteen minutes, she opens the oven door, removes her freshly made protein crust, and adds the new batter right on top of the crust while continuing to sing "Africa." She then puts the whole thing back in the oven.

She's washing the dishes next, hopping around to the sound of Toto's "Africa," and clearing the counters. She's putting stuff away: all her protein powder tubs, ingredients, and spoons. She approaches the fridge to put the milk back in. Then, suddenly (and dramatically), the music stops.

Zoom in on the woman picking up the shopping bag and looking inside. Then, slowly, zoom in on the woman's face looking at the camera.

Ominously, she whispers: "I forgot the eggs . . ."

CUT.

So, yeah! I made these bars without eggs. I totally forgot to add eggs until it was too late. But the bars turned out awesome! Super creamy and mmm, the combo of vanilla plus lemon is killer. Plus, the crust . . . the crust! I loved the crust. In fact, I'd like to recommend the crust for protein cheesecakes, too—it was crumbly, nutty, and yummmmm-oh. :-))))))

PROTEIN LEMON BARS

SERVINGS
6 bars

NUTRITIONAL DATA PER SERVING
154.1kcals, 9.8g protein, 10.85g carbs, 7g fat, 5.28g fiber

When you're zesting your own lemons, remember to use unwaxed, organic lemons or just give them a good scrub if you're not sure!

INGREDIENTS

CRUST

1 tablespoon coconut flour

6 tablespoons oat flour

1/4 cup vanilla whey protein powder

1 tablespoon pea protein powder (or vanilla casein protein powder)

1/4 cup almond milk (or regular)

4 Brazil nuts (could replace this with almonds)

1 tablespoon lemon zest

Freshly squeezed juice of 1/2 lemon

1 teaspoon vanilla sweetener liquid (or honey, agave, Splenda, or stevia—basically, your sweetener of choice)

FILLING

1 tablespoon lemon zest

Freshly squeezed juice of 1 lemon

1/2 cup vanilla whey protein powder

3 tablespoons coconut flour (or ground almonds)

15 macadamia nuts (could replace with cashews)

1/2 cup almond milk (again, you can replace this with any other milk)

TOPPING

2 tablespoons MCT powder or granulated stevia

DIRECTIONS

1. Preheat oven to 375°F (around 190°C).

2. Blend the crust ingredients together and press into a small cake pan.

3. Bake for about 10 minutes and remove from oven.

4. Meanwhile, make your filling by mixing all the ingredients together with an immersion blender, blender, or food processor. Spread this batter onto the hot crust and return bars to the oven for about 15–20 minutes (no longer).

5. Then, here's the touch of genius: Sprinkle some MCT powder or powdered stevia on top! It looks like powdered sugar, but, well, it's MCT power! Which is above-the-moon delicious and quite magical, too.

LOW-CARB PEANUT BUTTER & JELLY PROTEIN BARS

Well, well, well. I've done it. I didn't think it would be possible, but guess what. I did it. I created a really low-carb protein bar. And I ate it. Scrap that, I demolished it. I almost broke into cartwheels when I bit into it. This bar is just so delicious! And the macros are pretty wild, too. The bars are what they are thanks largely to two magical ingredients: (1) isomalto-oligosaccharides (a.k.a. IMO)—the secret of many low-carb protein foods out there, and (2) peanut butter & jelly flavoring powder.

SERVINGS
2 bars
NUTRITIONAL DATA PER SERVING
162kcals, 16g protein, 4g carbs, 8g fat

INGREDIENTS
1 tablespoon IMO syrup
1/4 cup unflavored whey protein powder
2 tablespoons ground almonds
1 tablespoon smooth peanut butter
1/2 teaspoon PB & J flavoring powder
1 1/2 teaspoons water

DIRECTIONS
1. First, heat up your IMO in a pot or pan until it bubbles.

2. Then add all the remaining ingredients to the pot and mix it until you get a sort of soft, warm dough.

3. Take this dough off the heat, transfer it to a cookie sheet lined with parchment paper or wax paper, and mold it into two small bars or one big one.

4. Put it in the freezer for 30 minutes and . . . voilà! Soft and gooey peanut butter & jelly low-carb protein bars!

HONEY HONEY PROTEIN BARS

"Hey, could you make me some breakfast bars to eat when I get to work?"

"Sure! What kind would you like?"

"Well, something a bit higher carb since I'll be eating them after my cycle into work. Oh, and if you can add some seeds in there, that'd be great!"

"How about some seeded honey protein bars?"

"Perfect! With dark chocolate on the outside?"

"And maybe some honeycomb for extra crunch!"

INGREDIENTS

1 tablespoon honey
3/4 cup milk (I use coconut, but any will do)
1/4 cup rolled oats (gluten-free or regular)
1/2 cup vanilla pea protein powder (or casein protein powder)
3 tablespoons date syrup (or agave or more honey)
1 tablespoon coconut flour
1 tablespoon pumpkin seeds, sunflower seeds, or flaxseeds
1 tablespoon honeycomb
1/2 bar (50g) 85 percent dark chocolate

DIRECTIONS

1. Mix all ingredients together in a bowl (except for the chocolate) and mold into four bars. If your mix is too crumbly, add more liquid. If it's too wet, add a bit more protein powder or coconut flour.

2. Once all bars are formed, melt the chocolate and dip the bars in there.

3. Then transfer them to the freezer for an hour or to the fridge for three, and BAAAAM, you're done. :-)

SERVINGS
4 bars
NUTRITIONAL DATA PER SERVING
183.25kcals, 15.5g protein, 20g carbs, 5g fat, 5g fiber

APRICOT & PISTACHIO PROTEIN TRUFFLES

SERVINGS

10 truffles

NUTRITIONAL DATA PER SERVING

55.34kcals, 4g protein, 4g carbs, 2.1g fat, 2.8g fiber

INGREDIENTS

1/4 cup vanilla rice protein powder

1 tablespoon applesauce

2 tablespoons psyllium husks

1 tablespoon vanilla stevia

3/4 cup almond milk

2 tablespoons coconut flour (or ground almonds)

3 tablespoons ground pistachio nuts, divided

3 tablespoons low-sugar apricot jam

DIRECTIONS

1. Mix all ingredients together (except for 1/2 of the nuts and the jam) until you get a doughy mix that you can roll with your hands.

2. Once your mix is nice and doughy, divide it into ten little balls, flatten them out in the palm of your hand, add some jam in the center, and roll them up. If you want to skip over this step, just roll the truffles without the jam and add the jam on top afterward. It's always good to have a "two left hands" option handy. :-)

3. Roll the truffles in the remaining pistachio nuts. You can also roll them in grated coconut or chopped almonds or pretty much whatever you like. Cocoa is quite nice with truffles, but here I didn't use cocoa because I find the combination of chocolate and fruit unpleasant, so . . . yeah. Anyhow, that's it: boom—done. Finito!

WHOA, WHOA, WHOA PROTEIN-FILLED DARK TRUFFLES

I made these truffles using saffron. Now, if you don't want to buy any saffron (it can be kind of expensive), you CAN omit it and just make some vanilla-filled chocolates instead. Please, please do keep the orange rind, though—it's marvelous! And consider adding some cinnamon and/or extra cocoa? Mmmmm. :-)

By "saffron water" I mean water that has been infused with saffron. The way you make it is by boiling 1/4 cup of water, putting a strand of saffron in there, and letting it soak until your water becomes deep yellow (around five minutes). The longer you leave it in there, the stronger your saffron water will be. :-) Give it a stir with a spoon to hurry up the process.

SERVINGS

10 truffles

NUTRITIONAL DATA PER SERVING

51kcals, 3.4g protein, 2.3g carbs, 2.95g fat, 1.9g fiber

INGREDIENTS

2 tablespoons vanilla custard whey protein powder

1/2 cup Greek yogurt

2 tablespoons saffron water

1 tablespoon probiotic vanilla premium peptide

2 tablespoons canned chickpeas

1 heaping tablespoon coconut flour

1 tablespoon vanilla stevia

1 tablespoon orange rind

1/2 bar (50g) 85 percent dark chocolate

DIRECTIONS

1. Blend everything together using a food processor or immersion blender until a paste or soft dough is formed. Then roll it into ten little balls and place on a cookie sheet lined with parchment paper or wax paper. For best results, chill balls for 20–30 minutes in the refrigerator.

2. Meanwhile, melt chocolate as described on page 141. Dip or coat balls in chocolate and return them to the parchment-lined cookie sheet. Place in the freezer or refrigerator until chocolate has hardened, and . . . BOOM! Done. :-)

CRUNCHY BANANA PROTEIN CHOCOLATES

The idea for this came to me when I was walking down an aisle of Whole Foods and found almost an entire shelf full of freeze-dried fruit. Waaa! A bag of bananas just jumped into my basket. When I got home, I opened it and made these chocolates. They're really easy to make! And so yummy. Check it out.

SERVINGS
6 chocolates

NUTRITIONAL DATA
51kcals, 3.4g protein, 2.3g carbs, 2.95g fat, 1.9g fiber

INGREDIENTS
1/4 cup vanilla (or banana) whey protein powder

1/4 cup coconut flour

3 tablespoons peanut butter

1/8–1/4 cup coconut milk (use enough to bind all the ingredients together)

6 freeze-dried banana slices

About 1/2 bar (40g) dark chocolate

DIRECTIONS
1. Mix together all the ingredients (except the banana slices and the chocolate), using a fork. Using a fork is better than using a blender, because the mixture will be sticky, and you don't want to end up with a ton of it stuck to the bottom of the blender).

2. When it's pasty and dry enough to shape, divide the mixture into six balls, and put a freeze-dried banana slice in the center of each as you roll it into a ball (if it's too wet or sticky to shape, just add a bit more coconut flour; if your mix is too crumbly, add a bit more milk).

3. Place the balls on a cookie sheet lined with parchment paper or wax paper. For best results, chill balls for 20–30 minutes in the refrigerator (optional).

4. Then melt chocolate as described on page 141. Dip or coat balls in chocolate and return them to the parchment-lined cookie sheet. Place in freezer or refrigerator until chocolate has hardened.

5. Take them out. Bite in. Feel the crunch of the banana. The softness of the chocolate. The peanut-buttery-ness and vanilla yumminess of the filling. Ooooooooooooooooo la la la. :-D

BLACK ONYX TRUFFLES

Black Onyx. It sounds like a superhero's archenemy, doesn't it? A sort of villain? Well, sadly, it's not (yet). It's a kind of cocoa powder. A really good and intense kind of cocoa powder. It's deep black because it's extremely alkalized. It also has less fat than regular cocoa powder. Let me try to describe what black onyx cocoa powder tastes like: it's rich, woody, cinnamony, with a bit of subtle licorice that complements the depth of the cocoa to perfection.

Now, if you don't have or can't get black onyx, you can still make this recipe. Just use regular cocoa powder. But the onyx . . . fwaaaa—try it if you can. Use it for the Protein "Oreo" cookies as well (see page 197)!

SERVINGS
4 truffles
NUTRITIONAL DATA PER SERVING
90kcals, 5g protein, 4g carbs, 7g fat

INGREDIENTS
1 tablespoon black onyx cocoa powder
1/4 cup ground almonds
1/2 teaspoon vanilla sweetener
2 tablespoons chocolate whey protein powder
About 1/2 bar (40g) 85 percent dark chocolate

DIRECTIONS
1. Blend everything except chocolate together using a food processor or immersion blender until a paste or soft dough is formed. Then roll it into four little balls and place on a cookie sheet lined with parchment paper or wax paper. For best results, chill balls for 20–30 minutes in the refrigerator.

2. Meanwhile, melt chocolate as described on page 141. Dip or coat balls in chocolate and return them to the parchment-lined cookie sheet. Place in the freezer or refrigerator until chocolate has hardened, and . . . BOOM! Done. :-)

PEANUT BUTTER & MARSHMALLOW PROTEIN CUPS

When I make this recipe, I get a similar reaction from everyone who tastes them. It's the same each and every time—an initial calmness followed by shock, intense pleasure, and complete and utter disbelief. It sounds like this:

"Holy #?&$@! Anna!!!!! MMM!!!! These are BETTER than regular peanut butter cups! Anna, do you realize what you've just made here? And they're healthy?! Can I have another one?"

SERVINGS
6 chocolate cups
NUTRITIONAL DATA PER SERVING
123kcals, 9g protein, 4g carbs, 7g fat, 1g fiber

INGREDIENTS
1/2 cup peanut butter & marshmallow whey protein powder (or vanilla)
1 tablespoon peanut butter
2 tablespoons coconut flour
1/4 cup almond milk
About 1/2 bar (40g) 85-percent dark chocolate

DIRECTIONS
1. First, melt half of the chocolate as described on page 141.

2. Pour the chocolate into six mini muffin cups, spreading it around so there's some on the bottom and also on the sides. Stick them in the freezer for 10 minutes.

3. Meanwhile, make your filling by mixing all the remaining ingredients together.

4. Take the muffin cups out of the freezer and fill them with your protein filling. Press it down.

5. Now melt the rest of the chocolate and pour it over the filling.

6. Stick them in the freezer for 30–40 minutes. Done!

PROTEIN PUMPKIN CUPS

This recipe is a bit unusual, but I think it works because it yields these mini cups that are a cross between pumpkin pie and cake. They also have a bit of puddingness to them, in that they're creamy and moist inside. I really don't know how else to describe them! They just kind of straddle the border between a lot of different types of dessert. Try them and see for yourself.

SERVINGS
4 pie cups

NUTRITIONAL DATA PER SERVING
99kcals, 12g protein, 12g carbs, 2g fat, 9g fiber

INGREDIENTS

BASE

2 tablespoons oat flour

1 tablespoon vanilla pea or brown rice protein powder

3 tablespoons milk

FILLING

3/4 cup pumpkin puree

1/4 cup pumpkin pie–flavored whey protein powder, or a whey protein and egg protein powder blend

1/2 cup liquid egg whites

DIRECTIONS

1. Preheat oven to 325°F (around 160°C).

2. Blend the base ingredients together and press the batter inside four muffin cups. Then blend all the filling ingredients together and top the base layer with that.

3. Bake until the pies cook on top but are slightly wet in the center (about 25–30 minutes). Make sure you don't overbake them—the point is to keep them pie-like in texture, so as soon as the top cooks and they look done, remove them from the oven and let them cool.

RASPBERRY & VANILLA PROTEIN CHOCOLATES

These protein chocolates are outwardly crunchy from the chocolate shell and inwardly crunchy from the raspberries and nuts.

SERVINGS

12 chocolates

NUTRITIONAL DATA PER SERVING

134kcals, 8g protein, 5g carbs, 8g fat

INGREDIENTS

1/2 cup vanilla whey protein powder

1/2 cup coconut flour

1/2 cup chopped walnuts

1/2 cup chopped almonds

1/2 cup cottage cheese

1/2 cup raspberries (fresh or frozen)

1/4 cup water

1/2 bar (50g) 85 percent dark chocolate

DIRECTIONS

1. Blend all ingredients together except the dark chocolate, shape the batter into twelve balls, and place on a cookie sheet lined with parchment paper or wax paper. For best results, chill bars for 20–30 minutes in the refrigerator (optional).

2. Meanwhile, melt chocolate as described on page 141. Dip or coat balls in chocolate and return them to the parchment-lined cookie sheet. Place in the freezer or refrigerator until chocolate has hardened, BOOOM! Finito. :-D

VANILLA-FILLED PROTEIN CHOCOLATES

Protein-filled chocolates are a great gift to give to your healthy friends and loved ones, especially if you put them in a nice wrapped box! I make these with different fillings every year for Valentine's Day. You'll need a silicone chocolate mold with around 16 cups, though you can always make them bigger or smaller as you wish.

SERVINGS

16 chocolates

NUTRITIONAL DATA PER SERVING

65kcals, 5g protein, 3g carbs (out of which 2g is fiber so net carbs = 1g!), 4g fat

INGREDIENTS

1 bar (100g) dark chocolate

1/2 cup vanilla whey protein powder (you can play with the flavor, anything will work}

2 tablespoons coconut flour

1/2 cup milk (almond or coconut would be best)

2 tablespoons ground almonds

2 tablespoons cashew, peanut, or almond butter

1 teaspoon flavoring or extract (I like caramel with vanilla whey, but anything goes)

DIRECTIONS

1. Melt chocolate as described on page 141. Pour about half of it into the individual cups in the mold (should make about 16, depending on the size of each one). Set the remaining chocolate aside.

2. Spread the chocolate to cover the bottom and sides of each of the mold holes you're using, and put in the freezer for about 15 minutes or until the chocolate sets.

3. Meanwhile, mix all of the above ingredients together (except for the chocolate bar) in a big bowl until a soft dough is formed. Add more coconut flour if the mixture seems too wet, or more milk if it seems too dry.

4. Take the mold out of the freezer and add your protein filling to it.

5. Warm the remaining chocolate until melted, and pour on top of each cup, thereby "sealing" your chocolates and "encasing" the filling inside them.

Make sure you try your batters for the bars and chocolates, to ensure it hits all the right notes. Word of warning: you WILL feel tempted to, at this stage, eat all the batter. Please don't. Think about how nice it will be to have a portable protein snack for later.

PROTEIN
BROWNIES
BLONDIES

WHEN I WAS GROWING UP IN CHICAGO, MY FAMILY AND I DIDN'T EAT OUT MUCH.

We just preferred to eat at home. Both my mom and dad were amazing cooks and loved to show off their cooking skills, so, really, there was no reason to venture outside for our meals.

Every once in a while, though, the urge for something different would strike, and . . . we'd go to a local steakhouse. My dad and brother would order ribs, my mom would go for chicken, and I'd order a cream of onion soup as my starter and a bowl of French onion soup as my main course (I know, what a weirdo, but what can I say? I loved my onions).

Anyway, when the waitress would come around with the dessert menu, my brother and I would always say yes and split something. Usually, that something was their chocolate fudge brownie with vanilla ice cream and chocolate sauce. Now, I remember this dessert being ridiculous—hot rich brownie, cold melting vanilla ice cream, mmmm. But I also remember getting really aggressive when it showed up on our table. I'd get my fork ready, and as soon as it hit the table, BAAAM! I'd go for it. My poor little brother would then just pout and get all angry. "Mom! Dad! She ate all of it!" But I'd smile ear to ear, stuffed to the brim, face full of chocolate. Don't blame me! I'd think. Blame love! Because I simply loved that dessert. It did crazy things to my spirit of sharing.

It was just really tasty. And it's exactly that which inspired me to make THIS dessert, a dessert that packs the same amount of nommage, the same level of intensity, and the same desire to absolutely destroy the plate—with one-tenth the calories, hardly any fat, no sugar, and a massive punch of protein POW! It's not sorcery, I promise.

LOW-CARB PROTEIN BROWNIES WITH VANILLA PROTEIN ICE CREAM

SERVINGS

4 brownies

NUTRITIONAL DATA PER SERVING

118kcals, 14g protein, 4g carbs, 4g fat

INGREDIENTS

1/4 cup coconut flour

1/4 cup chocolate whey protein powder

3/4 cup liquid egg whites

3 tablespoons cocoa powder

1 tablespoon vanilla stevia (or your sweetener of choice)

1/2 cup almond milk

1 tablespoon peanut butter for topping (optional but delicious!)

1/3 bar (30g) melted dark chocolate for topping
(optional but, come on—it's chocolate!)

DIRECTIONS

1. Preheat oven to 325°F (around 160°C).

2. Using an immersion blender, blender, or food processor, blend all ingredients together, except the peanut butter and the melted chocolate.

3. Pour into a small brownie pan (if you want to bake it in a medium or large one, make sure you double or even triple the recipe). Bake for about 30–35 minutes or until a knife inserted into the middle comes out clean. Make sure you don't overbake it, because if you do, it'll turn out dry and kind of weirdly crumbly; so just keep an eye on it.

4. Slice into squares and add a scoop of protein ice cream on top (see pages 242 and 243)!

5. Pour some peanut butter on top of the ice cream. You can pour some melted dark chocolate, too, or even almond butter. I just like adding peanut butter because the one I use is super creamy and contains just one ingredient: peanuts. This step is optional, though.

PEANUT BUTTER & DARK CHOCOLATE PROTEIN BROWNIES

These brownies are a nutritional powerhouse! They're full of vitamins, minerals, antioxidants, essential fatty acids (including omega-3s), protein, and fiber goodness. They're also vegan, gluten-free, and sweetener-free. I made them this way because I've been asked to create more sweetener-free and egg-free protein recipes by people who either don't react well to sweeteners or eggs or who just prefer not to include them in their diet. I actually like to create vegan recipes every now and then and frequently upload them on proteinpow. com. Cooking within different parameters allows me to be more creative in my cooking and play with different kinds of protein foods, so . . . yeah! Bring it on!

SERVINGS

9 brownies

NUTRITIONAL DATA PER SERVING

133.8kcals, 8.4g protein, 16.5g carbs, 4.5g fat

INGREDIENTS

1 tablespoon smooth peanut butter

1/2 cup chocolate hemp protein powder

1/4 cup pumpkin puree (or cooked sweet potato)

2 tablespoons chocolate pea protein powder

1 banana

10 medjool dates

2 tablespoons apple fiber (or coconut flour)

1/4 cup buckwheat flour (or oat flour)

1/2 teaspoon baking soda

1 1/4 cups coconut milk (or your nut milk of choice)

1/4 cup cocoa powder

DIRECTIONS

1. Preheat oven to 325°F (around 160°C).

2. Blend all ingredients together and taste your batter. If you want it sweeter, add more dates (just bear in mind this'll increase the carb content of your brownies). If you want it even more cocoa-ful, add more cocoa. If your batter is too dry, add a bit more milk. If it's too wet, dry it up with more pea protein powder or coconut flour.

3. Pour into a brownie pan and bake for about 35–45 minutes, or until a knife inserted into the middle comes out clean.

4. Let cool and then slice into squares. I sliced them into nine large brownie squares, but you could always slice them smaller if, for instance, you want bite-size brownies.

FENNEL & PUMPKIN DARK CHOCOLATE PROTEIN BROWNIES

A few months ago, I was out at a food festival chatting with a well-known professional chef. There, I asked him about his favorite flavor combinations and he recommended adding fennel to all things chocolate. That's one combination that would never have crossed my mind, so I asked him how he went about mixing the two. "Just toast the fennel seeds a bit so they release some of their oil, grind them into a powder, and then add them to your chocolate. It's amazing!" he said. Needless to say, I was intrigued. I love unusual chocolate combinations, and fennel plus chocolate did sound amazing. That's what inspired me to create these dark chocolate fennel brownies, and I've got to say they are spectaaaacular! Topped with a tablespoon of cream, these brownies are really tasty. Please try them, with or without the cream. They turned out a bit overly moist (blame the copious amount of pumpkin, and my lack of proper flour in there), but oy, they are tasty! The fennel and chocolate combination is simply magical, out of this world. We're talking about a match made in heaven! Fennel and chocolate. Who would have thought, right?

Variations: If you don't have hemp but want to make them anyway, use chocolate pea protein powder or a yummy chocolate rice protein powder. If you don't have pea or rice and don't mind de-veganizing the brownies, try using casein protein powder along with one or two egg whites.

SERVINGS
8 brownies
NUTRITIONAL DATA PER SERVING
132.8kcals, 12.5g protein, 10.1g carbs, 4.4g fat, 7.6g fiber

INGREDIENTS
4 small cooked beets (boiled or roasted), unsalted
3 tablespoons coconut flour
1 cup chocolate hemp protein powder
1 1/4 cups pumpkin puree
1/2 cup cocoa powder
1 tablespoon ground fennel seed
1 1/2 teaspoons toffee flavdrops
        (or your sweetener of choice)

DIRECTIONS
1. Preheat oven to 325°F (around 160°C).

2. Using an immersion blender, blender, or food processor, blend all the above ingredients together.

3. Taste the batter. Do you want it sweeter? Add more flavdrops or your sweetener of choice. Do you want it more chocolatey? Add more cocoa. Is it absolutely spot-on? Try not to eat it all.

4. Pour into a brownie pan and bake for about 40–60 minutes, or until a knife inserted into the middle comes out clean. Just keep an eye on it.

CHESTNUT & DARK CHOCOLATE PROTEIN BROWNIE CAKE

I made these brownies during a particularly dark week where all we got was darkness and rainclouds accompanied by freezing gusts of wind. To take a stance against the dismal weather, I decided to make a sunny-looking cake. I wanted something to enjoy alongside my morning cup of tea before I geared up and braved the elements on my way to the gym. This cake was it!

SERVINGS

12 slices

NUTRITIONAL DATA PER SERVING

79kcals, 7g protein, 6g carbs, 2g fat, 3.3g fiber

INGREDIENTS

1/2 cup chocolate hemp protein powder

2 beets (boiled or roasted), unsalted

3/4 cup liquid egg whites

3 tablespoons cocoa powder

1 tablespoon pea protein powder

1/2 cup chestnut flour

1 cup hemp milk

1/4 cup coconut flour

1 tablespoon toffee flavoring drops or your sweetener of choice

Sunflower seed butter for topping (optional)

Strawberries for topping (optional)

DIRECTIONS

1. Preheat oven to 325°F (around 160°C).

2. Using an immersion blender, blender, or food processor, blend all ingredients together (except the berries and seed butter, if you're using them).

3. Pour mixture into a loaf pan and bake for about 40–45 minutes, or until a knife inserted into the middle comes out clean.

4. Let it cool and then cut the loaf into twelve slices.

5. Grab two of them, top them with sunflower seed butter and strawberries, and well, well, well. . . . The end product is this soft, brownie-like, chestnut-y, and utterly delicious chocolate cake that opens up the clouds and brings in the sunshine!

SWEET POTATO & NUTELLA PROTEIN BROWNIES

Welcome to a recipe that exists beyond the realm of introduction.

SERVINGS
6 brownies

NUTRITIONAL DATA PER SERVING
114.85kcals, 9.6g protein, 11.2g carbs, 3.1g fat, 2.7g fiber

INGREDIENTS

1 large sweet potato, oven-roasted and unsalted

1/2 cup chocolate whey protein powder

2 tablespoons coconut flour

2 eggs

1/2 teaspoon baking powder

1 tablespoon Nutella, plus more for filling

DIRECTIONS

1. Preheat oven to 350°F (around 175°C).

2. Using an immersion blender, blender, or food processor, blend all the ingredients together.

3. Pour into a brownie pan and bake for about 35–45 minutes, or until a knife inserted into the middle comes out clean.

4. Let the brownies cool and cut into squares. Slice each square horizontally, add more Nutella (or nut butter), and boom! Get ready to dig into deliciousness!

BLUEBERRY & GOJI BERRY CHOCOLATE PROTEIN BROWNIES

There's something about berries and chocolate—particularly goji berries and/or blueberries and dark chocolate—that brings out the ridiculous in me. I mean, every recipe I've built around berries and chocolate is described with hyperbole and excessive adulation. My weakness for berries and chocolate is far from discreet; it's unmistakably hardcore. If you've tried the goji and chocolate combination, you'll know why I go gaga over it. It's just . . . wa, wa, wa!

SERVINGS
6 brownies

NUTRITIONAL DATA PER SERVING
139kcals, 11.7g protein, 12g carbs, 4.2g fat, 4.7g fiber

INGREDIENTS
1/2 cup coconut milk

1 tablespoon coconut flour

1/4 cup fresh blueberries

1/4 cup dried goji berries

1/2 cup chocolate hemp protein powder (or chocolate pea or rice protein powder)

1 egg

3 egg whites

1/4 cup instant buckwheat

2 tablespoons cocoa powder

2 tablespoons pea protein powder

1 tablespoon toffee flavdrops or your sweetener of choice

DIRECTIONS
1. Preheat oven to 325°F (around 160°C).

2. Using an immersion blender, blender, or food processor, blend all the above ingredients together.

3. Pour mixture into a brownie pan and bake for about 40 minutes, or until a knife inserted into the middle comes out clean.

4. Let it cool and then cut into six brownies.

MEXICAN CHOCOLATE PROTEIN BROWNIE BITES

I made these brownies on a day we were having our new neighbors over for tea. I figured, what better way to introduce powder-skeptics (i.e., people who've never had protein powders and are suspicious of their origin and composition) to the fantastic world of protein powder cooking than by making a batch of yuhmmmmay Mexican chocolate protein brownies? I decided to cut them into bite-size pieces, because I've learned that powder-skeptics are often a bit shocked by the protein kaboomness, so they must be introduced with care. Plus, by making them this size, I figured, more for everyone! You can, of course, divide them into however many pieces you want or . . . heck, you can add some casein frosting and turn the whole thing into a rich chocolate protein cake.

SERVINGS
1 batch
NUTRITIONAL DATA PER 1/10 BATCH
61.8kcals, 7.7g protein, 4.2g carbs, 1.8g fat, 2.4g fiber

INGREDIENTS
3/4 cup liquid egg whites
1/2 cup pumpkin puree (or cooked sweet potato)
2 tablespoons apple fiber (or psyllium husks)
6 tablespoons chocolate hemp protein powder
2 tablespoons cocoa powder
2 tablespoons chocolate pea protein powder
2 tablespoons chocolate brown rice protein powder
1 cup milk (I use coconut milk, but any will do)
1 teaspoon cinnamon
1/2 teaspoon red chili powder
Cocoa powder for sprinkling on top (optional)

DIRECTIONS
1. Preheat oven to 325°F (around 160°C).

2. Using an immersion blender, blender, or food processor, blend all the ingredients together, except the cocoa powder.

3. Bake for about 35 minutes, or until a knife inserted into the middle comes out clean.

4. Slice them into however many pieces you want. You can sprinkle them with cocoa powder, too. This is totally optional, but they look nicer with the cocoa, I think. :-)

DID YOU KNOW THAT THE INDUSTRIAL CULTIVATION OF HEMP CAN BE TRACED BACK THOUSANDS OF YEARS?

That the US Constitution was actually written on paper that was made out of hemp, or that George Washington apparently grew, used, and sold it? Did you know that, during World War II, US farmers were encouraged to grow hemp for cloth, cordage, and rope? Since the late 1950s, however, federal laws have prohibited its growth for commercial purposes. In fact, if you buy hemp protein powder in the US, it's probably coming from Canada, where hemp cultivation was legalized in 1997.

Hemp protein powder represents a complete source of essential fatty acids, and, in addition to vitamin A, calcium, phosphorous, iron, magnesium, and zinc, it contains a number of essential amino acids. But what makes me love it the most is that it bakes beautifully and goes amazingly well with chocolate. ;-)

HEMP BROWNIES (THE HIGH-PROTEIN LEGAL VERSION)

SERVINGS

9 brownies

NUTRITIONAL DATA PER SERVING

87.5kcals, 7.2g protein, 6.6g carbs, 2.9g fat, 3.8g fiber

INGREDIENTS

1 small cooked sweet potato (boiled or roasted until soft)

1/2 cup chocolate hemp protein powder

3 tablespoons organic cocoa powder

1/4 cup coconut flour

1 1/4 cups liquid egg whites

1 1/2 cups almond milk

1/2 teaspoon baking soda

1 small zucchini, grated

DIRECTIONS

1. Preheat oven to 325°F (around 160°C).

2. Using an immersion blender, blender, or food processor, blend together all the above ingredients except the zucchini.

3. Press your grated zucchini onto a napkin to remove excess liquid, and then fold it into your batter.

4. Pour the mixture into a silicone brownie pan.

5. Bake for 1 hour and 15–20 minutes, or until a knife inserted into the middle comes out clean.

6. Take them out, let them cool, and be ready to experience soft and extreme deliciousness on your plate, napkin, or hand. Because of all the milk in there, the brownies turn out extremely moist and chocolatey, so that they melt in your mouth in a boom, boom, boom sort of way!

ALMOND, VANILLA & ORANGE PROTEIN BLONDIES

Blondies are kind of like brownies but without the chocolate. They deliver the same KAPOW! that brownies do, but their punch is lighter. Blondies usually feature, shall we say, "opulent" amounts of butter, and you'll often find them with nuts—especially almonds, walnuts, and macadamia nuts—and sometimes even chocolate chips (though to me that's blurring the divide between them and their brown counterparts a little too openly). I'll be making more protein blondies in the future, because they're delicious and oh so full of goodness.

SERVINGS

8 blondies

NUTRITIONAL DATA PER SERVING

84kcals, 8.6g protein, 4g carbs, 3.4g fat, 2.4g fiber

INGREDIENTS

3/4 cup canned pumpkin puree (or 3/4 cup mashed sweet potato)

1/2 cup liquid egg whites

1 egg yolk

1/2 cup pea protein powder

2 tablespoons coconut flour

1/2 cup slivered almonds (plus extra for garnish)

1 tablespoon toffee flavdrops or your sweetener of choice

1 tablespoon vanilla extract

1 teaspoon grated orange zest

DIRECTIONS

1. Preheat oven to 325°F (around 160°C).

2. Blend all ingredients together and pour the batter into a small brownie pan, adding some additional slivered almonds on top (this is optional but adds a great texture dimension to the whole thing).

3. Bake for about 40–50 minutes, or until a knife inserted into the middle comes out clean.

4. Slice into squares, or if you like to dip things in coffee, as I do, you can slice them into rectangles.

5. They're absolutely beautiful soaked with coffee, wohohoa!

VANILLA PROTEIN BLONDIES

My aim here was to create something overwhelmingly vanilla-y. That's all I had in mind, and this is what came out of the oven. Madness. What can I say? I wanted vanilla, and boooom! These blondies most certainly delivered that, and then some. Ahhhh! The texture was absolutely surreal. . . . I like to eat mine with almond butter.

SERVINGS
6 blondies

NUTRITIONAL DATA PER SERVING
103kcals, 9.4g protein, 6.2g carbs, 3.8g fat, 1g fiber

INGREDIENTS
1/4 cup ground almonds

1/4 cup vanilla pea protein powder

1/4 cup whole milk

1 egg

4 egg whites

1/2 cup rolled oats (gluten-free or regular)

1/2 cup vanilla casein protein powder

1 teaspoon chicory powder (optional)

1 tablespoon plus 1 teaspoon coconut flour

1/2 teaspoon baking soda

DIRECTIONS
1. Preheat oven to 325°F (around 160°C).

2. Using an immersion blender, blender, or food processor, blend all the above ingredients together.

3. Pour into a brownie pan and bake for about 40–45 minutes, or until a knife inserted into the middle comes out clean.

4. Let the blondies cool and cut into squares.

IT HAS BEEN A LONG AND ARDUOUS JOURNEY TO THESE COOKIES. MY JOURNEY TO FIND THE PERFECT PROTEIN COOKIE RECIPE BEGAN IN 2009.

I cannot even begin to tell you how many protein cookies I've made and thrown out, how many protein cookies have made me disappointed, how many protein cookies have led to this expression—an expression of "Meh, they're okay . . . not good, not bad."

Let me tell you: A LOT of cookies, more than I can count. But here it is. I present to you (drumroll) the best low-carb protein cookies on earth!

LOW-CARB PEANUT BUTTER PROTEIN COOKIES

SERVINGS

7 cookies

NUTRITIONAL DATA PER SERVING

150kcals, 22g protein, 2g carbs, 6g fat

INGREDIENTS

2 heaping tablespoons peanut butter

1/4 cup vanilla whey protein powder

1/4 cup coconut milk

1/4 cup ground almonds

1/4 cup vanilla pea protein powder

DIRECTIONS

1. Preheat oven to 350°F (around 175°C).

2. Mix together all your ingredients until a dough is formed.

3. Grab chunks of this dough and shape seven balls out of it. Put these balls onto a cookie sheet lined with parchment paper or silicone. Now press them down with a fork, the bottom of a glass, or, as I like to do, use a cookie stamp!

4. Bake the cookies for about 10 minutes, or until when you press them, they feel soft but cooked inside.

The final product is out-of-this-world delicious. The cookies are soft, crumbly, peanut butter-y, and fwaaaa. . . . I just don't know what to say. You have to make them. HAVE to make them. I do warn you, though, that they go quickly. So practice your sharing spirit and make sure you save some for your loved ones. Same with the batter—try not to eat it all. I ate one cookie's worth of batter before baking and had to mobilize strong reserves of self-control not to munch the rest!

WHEY PROTEIN COOKIES

Now, when you see the list of ingredients, you may think, "Apple and beans in cookies?! What the hell!?" And to that I say, I know. I know it's weird. But man ohhhh . . . man, do they work! I'll tell you why: the beans and the apple offset the whey's natural tendency to make cookies dry and/or rubbery. They add body to the cookies, and they do this without giving the cookie any apple or (God forbid) butter bean or chickpea undertones. The final product is gorgeous, oat-y, and light. You've just GOT to try this!

SERVINGS

8 cookies

NUTRITIONAL DATA PER SERVING

90kcals, 6.65g protein, 9.4g carbs, 2.8g fat, 1.8g fiber

You can add 1 tablespoon of vanilla stevia to the batter if you like your cookies extra sweet. You can also add a tablespoon of peanut butter to make them peanut butter-y and hhhhnnng. This goes for any of these recipes.

INGREDIENTS

1 egg

1/4 cup vanilla whey protein powder

1/2 apple, cored

1/4 cup cooked butter beans or chickpeas, rinsed and drained

2 tablespoons hulled hemp seeds
     (or ground almonds or flaxseeds)

1/2 teaspoon baking soda

1/2 cup rolled oats (gluten-free or regular)

DIRECTIONS

1. Preheat oven to 375°F (around 190°C).

2. Blend together all ingredients except the oats, using an immersion blender, blender, or food processor.

3. Once blended, add the oats in and whisk the mixture. You do this because you want to keep the oats whole, not mush them up with the rest of the stuff.

4. Spoon eight blobs of batter onto a cookie sheet lined with parchment paper or silicone and bake until the cookies have browned on top (15–25 minutes).

ANNA'S PROTEIN COOKIES

Cookies are great! You can pack them up and take them with you as a snack, stick them in a jar with a bow and give them as a gift, eat them with coffee, eat them with tea, crumble them up over some protein fluff or ice cream, etc., etc. Here's a recipe to get your protein powder cookie season going, for cookies that I couldn't figure out how to name, so I named them Anna's Protein Cookies because I love them.

Result? Lovely. :-D They're kind of bready and absolutely delish, especially when topped with some nut butter. You can actually also use them to sandwich some nut butter, so, you know, cookie on one side, nut butter, and then cookie again. I shared them with some friends that way, and they absolutely loved them! So I suggest you give them a shot, for sure. :-)

SERVINGS
16 cookies
NUTRITIONAL DATA PER SERVING
53.6kcals, 5.87g protein, 5g carbs, 1g fat, 2g fiber

INGREDIENTS
1 cup liquid egg whites

1/2 cup vanilla pea protein powder

2 tablespoons buckwheat flour (or oat flour)

2 tablespoons date syrup

1/4 cup rolled oats (gluten-free or regular) or buckwheat flakes

1/4 cup mix of pumpkin and sunflower seeds

2 tablespoons goji berries

DIRECTIONS

1. Preheat oven to 325°F (around 160°C).

2. Blend together all the above ingredients using an immersion blender, blender, or food processor.

3. Spoon batter onto a cookie sheet lined with parchment paper or silicone. You should get sixteen cookies altogether.

4. Bake for about 25–30 minutes, or until they're cooked through.

5. Done. If you want to "crunch them up" further, just flash grill them (i.e., stick them under the broiler for 3–4 minutes on each side and watch them so they don't burn) and booom: done.

THESE COOKIES ARE A CROSS BETWEEN CHOCOLATE CHIP COOKIES AND COOKIE DOUGH.

They're soft and gooey, and if you eat them fresh out of the oven, the dark chocolate just pours out, and you kind of die a little.

I wasn't planning on eating them like this—underbaked. I just didn't have the patience to wait for them to fully cook (post-workout appetite can sometimes do that to a person). So I took them out too early. I actually took them out planning to just "sample" one before putting the tray back in the oven, but when I sampled one of the cookies, I thought, "OLYMPUS! WHAT IS THIS?!" So I left the tray out, and my sense of restraint went out the window. I ate three of them, along with a glass of milk.

They're kind of revolutionary, these cookies. You could also say they're paleo, as they're totally grain- and dairy- free.

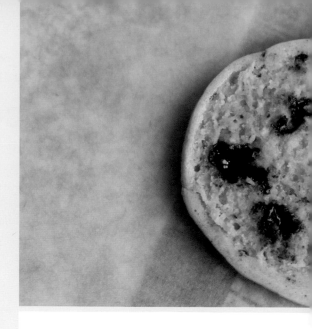

CHOCOLATE CHIP COOKIE DOUGH PROTEIN COOKIES

SERVINGS

8 cookies

NUTRITIONAL DATA PER SERVING

92kcals, 8g protein, 4g carbs, 5g fat

INGREDIENTS

1 small banana

1 egg

1/4 cup ground almonds

1 tablespoon peanut butter

1/2 cup vanilla beef–and–egg white protein powder

1 teaspoon chocolate chip flavoring or cocoa powder

1/5 bar (20g) dark chocolate (85 percent or higher),
        broken into small pieces

DIRECTIONS

1. Preheat oven to 350˚F (around 175˚C).

2. Blend together all the ingredients, except the chocolate pieces, using an immersion blender, blender, or food processor. Add your chocolate pieces at the end.

3. Use a spoon to plop them onto a cookie sheet lined with parchment paper or silicone.

4. Cook them for about 25–30 minutes, or until when you press them with your finger, they feel cooked.

5. At this stage you can either remove them from the oven using a spatula OR you can keep cooking to allow them to transform into proper cookies. I leave that decision to you and your taste buds.

LET ME BEGIN BY THUNDER-BOLTING YOU WITH A SURPRISING FACT: OREOS ARE VEGAN.

Yup. They don't contain dairy. A lot of people find this surprising because they think the creamy center is dairy-based. I mean, it looks like cream and sugar, right? But it's just a combination of vegetable oils, flour, high-fructose corn syrup, starch, and sugaaah (yum!). As long as one isn't pigging out on them Cookie Monster-style, an Oreo (or several) won't necessarily hurt one's soul—or waistline. But . . . this is one of the best "healthy Oreo" recipes that's ever been created. I dare you to find a better one. Go ahead. Search. Search, but you won't find! Because this one blows all others out of the water. STRAIGHT out of the water. Like a meteor crashing into the ocean!

It's pretty wild. They're supremely easy to make and absolutely divine. I swear.

PROTEIN "OREOS"

SERVINGS

6 to 9 cookies

NUTRITIONAL DATA PER SERVING

73kcals, 4g protein, 6g carbs, 4g fat, 2.5g fiber

INGREDIENTS

COOKIE

2 tablespoons black cocoa powder

2 tablespoons unflavored brown rice protein powder

2 tablespoons tahini (or peanut butter)

1 tablespoon agave syrup

1 teaspoon honey

3 medjool dates

FILLING

1 tablespoon xylitol or your sweetener of choice

1 tablespoon coconut flour

3 tablespoons coconut milk (or almond milk)

2 tablespoons brown rice protein powder

1 teaspoon coconut oil

DIRECTIONS

1. Preheat oven to 375°F (around 190°C).

2. Blend together the cookie ingredients using an immersion blender, blender, or food processor.

3. Divide the mixture into twelve to eighteen little balls (depending on how big your muffin pans are) and flatten them on the bottom of twelve to eighteen silicone muffin cups.

4. Bake for about 10–15 minutes, or until they've cooked through.

5. Once your cookies have cooled, mix the filling ingredients together in a bowl until you get a creamy consistency. If your mixture is too crumbly, add a bit of water or coconut milk until your mixture becomes nice and thick.

6. Roll the filling out into six to nine little balls (depending on how many cookies you made) and sandwich each one between two cookie halves.

7. Feel the back of your shirt start to rip as the wings come through it and raise you up into the clouds of nommage!

DARK CHOCOLATE & MACADAMIA NUT PROTEIN COOKIES

These cookies are crunchy, crumbly, soft inside, and ohhhh, with the 100 percent dark chocolate and the macadamias in there, ahhh! They're almost sinful. I had one with my afternoon cup of coffee, and seriously almost began levitating in pleasure, up off my chair and straight through the ceiling, right up into the sky (assuming, of course, that my body would just go through the ceiling seamlessly). They're marvelous. Incidentally, they're also vegan!

SERVINGS

9 cookies

NUTRITIONAL DATA PER SERVING

120kcals, 10g protein, 7g carbs, 6.5g fat, 2g fiber

INGREDIENTS

3/4 cup vanilla brown rice protein powder

1 banana

1/2 cup coconut milk

2 tablespoons pea protein powder

1/4 cup rolled oats (gluten-free or regular)

1/4 cup hulled hemp seeds

1 tablespoon coconut oil

1/2 bar (50g) 100 percent dark chocolate, broken into small pieces

2 tablespoons chopped macadamia nuts

DIRECTIONS

1. Preheat oven to 375°F (around 190°C).

2. Blend together brown rice protein powder, banana, coconut milk, pea protein powder, oats, hemp seeds, and coconut oil.

3. Stir in the chocolate and the nuts.

4. Spoon batter into about nine cookies on a cookie sheet lined with parchment paper or silicone.

5. Bake for 15–20 minutes, or until cooked through.

DARK CHOCOLATE DIGESTIVES

These protein cookies (which, by the way, are gluten-free) turned out really well. Those of you unfamiliar with the British cookie (or "biscuit") scene are probably thinking that "digestives" is a strange and unappetizing name for cookies. Let me explain: I'm calling these Dark Chocolate Digestives not because of their digestibility (although, when you look at the first ingredient, you'll notice that the word digestive would probably not be irrelevant) but because they're exactly like actual digestive biscuits, only 100 percent better! Don't believe me? Try this recipe.

SERVINGS

12 cookies

NUTRITIONAL DATA PER SERVING

85kcals, 5g protein, 10.9g carbs, 3.2g fat, 3.3g fiber

INGREDIENTS

1 (15-ounce) can black beans, rinsed and drained

1/2 cup chocolate whey protein powder

1/2 cup liquid egg whites

1/2 cup buckwheat flakes

1/2 cup cocoa powder

1 tablespoon toffee flavdrops, liquid stevia, or your sweetener of choice

1 teaspoon sea salt

1 tablespoon fennel seeds (unusual, I know, but Zeus are they good here!)

1 bar (100g) dark chocolate

DIRECTIONS

1. Preheat oven to 325°F (around 160°C).

2. Blend all the above ingredients together (except the chocolate).

3. Pour mixture into four large muffin cups or six standard muffin cups.

4. Bake for about 10–20 minutes, depending on muffin size, or until fully cooked.

5. Meanwhile, melt chocolate as described on page 141.

6. Remove muffins from oven and let them cool. Slice them horizontally into rounds (three for the large ones, and in half for the small ones).

7. Spoon melted chocolate onto cookies.

8. Move them to the freezer, where they need to chill out for 30 minutes (to allow the chocolate to set). BOOM: THAT IS IT.

ONE DAY, A PROTEIN COOKIE MET A LOAF OF BANANA PROTEIN BREAD.

They quickly fell in love. They moved in together, and before long, they had offspring: Banana Bread Protein Cookies. Say hello! They are wonderful—crunchy on the outside and cakey on the inside.

When I first made them and they were nice and browned (and my entire house smelled of banana heaven), I took them out, let them cool, and walked myself over to the gym, where I had an annoying workout (thanks to a clown who kept getting in the way of my supersets). When I got home, I proceeded to pointlessly stick the cookies in a plastic bag before realizing I wanted to just eat them, so I ripped the bag open and munch, munch, munch. :-D

They were 100 percent like banana bread cookies. The wattleseeds (which, by the way, you can substitute pitted medjool dates for if you can't find them) added this terrific extra flavor dimension—a kind of roasted nuttiness that totally managed to capture the umph of the cookies, rounding out their character with gusto.

BANANA BREAD PROTEIN COOKIES

SERVINGS

9 cookies

NUTRITIONAL DATA PER SERVING

52kcals, 6g protein, 3.8g carbs, 1.2g fat, 1.6g fiber

INGREDIENTS

1 banana

1/2 cup banana or vanilla whey protein powder

2 tablespoons coconut flour

3/4 cup coconut milk

1 teaspoon banana extract

1 teaspoon granulated stevia

1 teaspoon roasted wattleseeds

    (or a couple of medjool dates)

DIRECTIONS

1. Preheat oven to 350°F (around 175°C).

2. Blend together all the above ingredients using an immersion blender, blender, or food processor.

3. With your spoon, form nine circular blobs on a silicone cookie sheet or one lined with parchment paper.

4. Bake for about 25–35 minutes, until brown.

DARK CHOCOLATE PEANUT BUTTER PROTEIN DONUTS

SERVINGS

36 (very) mini donuts or about 24 mini donuts

NUTRITIONAL DATA PER SERVING

20.4kcals, 2g protein, 1.1g carbs, 0.9g fat, 1g fiber

Have you ever eaten donuts as cereal? Floating in a bowl of milk to be eaten one by one with a spoon? I have, and I recommend it. :-D. On to the recipe. I've always been intrigued by peanut flour, and now I've used it. It lends a mild peanut-butteriness that's quite different from what you get from using good old peanut butter. These donuts are gorgeously cakey and dark chocolatey, with peanut-y undertones and BOOOM! A smooth outer shell of intensely rich dark chocolate power, boom baraboom!

INGREDIENTS

2 tablespoons sugar-free peanut flour
   or peanut butter flour
1 cup liquid egg whites
1 small beet, boiled, steamed,
   or roasted, unsalted
6 tablespoons chocolate
   hemp protein powder
1/4 cup coconut flour
1 tablespoon cocoa powder
1 cup coconut milk
1/10 bar (10g) dark chocolate

DIRECTIONS

1. Preheat oven to 325°F (around 160°C).

2. Using an immersion blender, blender, or food processor, blend together all the ingredients, except the chocolate.

3. Pour the batter into two mini donut trays (or do the process twice if you're using the same tray to make all 36 mini donuts), preferably silicone.

4. Bake for 10–15 minutes, or until a knife inserted into the middle comes out clean.

5. Massage the chocolate bar directly onto the warm donuts. It will melt and make a delicious topping.

6. Serve floating in a bowl of milk.

DARK CHOCOLATE PROTEIN COOKIES

The first thing I must mention is that the batter for these cookies is really good! I found myself in the middle of the kitchen licking the bowl while nommmmming like some kind of mistakenly discharged lunatic. It just made me realize that, unbaked, the mix below would make one hell of a delicious chocolate-pudding-type thing! So tasty . . . but I baked it—baked it into equally delicious dark chocolatey cookies. :-)

SERVINGS

9 cookies

NUTRITIONAL DATA PER SERVING

11.2g protein, 4g carbs, 2.9g fat, 3.8g fiber

INGREDIENTS

1/2 cup chocolate hemp protein powder

1 cup liquid egg whites

1/4 cup coconut flour

2 tablespoons cocoa powder

1/4 cup pea protein powder

1 1/4 cups milk

1 teaspoon toffee flavdrops, liquid stevia, or
    your sweetener of choice

DIRECTIONS

1. Preheat oven to 350˚F (around 175˚C).

2. Blend together all the ingredients using an immersion blender, blender, or food processor.

3. Carefully spoon out batter onto a cookie sheet. You should get about nine small cookies. Alternatively, use a muffin pan and spoon batter into about nine muffin cups.

4. Bake for 15–20 minutes. The secret here is not to overbake them. When they're in the oven, test them after 15–20 minutes—you want them soft in the center and almost crunchy on the outside. Oy, oy, oy . . . dunked in some good old-fashioned cow's milk? Mmmmm!

CHOCOLATE-COVERED PROTEIN PRETZELS

I know, I know. Pretzels are a complex food that involves yeast, flour, and dough-kneading and twisting action. Making pretzels takes skill, know-how, and time. They're not something you make on a whim, and especially not something you make without experience or technical knowledge. That's why most people buy pretzels instead of making them at home—they're too hard to make and far too much of a hassle to bother with. Right?

Wrong. Making pretzels is easy! Chocolate-covered protein ones at least.

All you need is a good dough and a pretzel cutter (you can get this online by simply searching for "pretzel cutter"). Ideally, you want to get a spring-loaded pretzel cutter. That way your dough can be more easily released from its mold after it's shaped into a pretzel. After you cook them and dip them in chocolate, you can sprinkle the tops with chocolate flakes, honeycomb, or strawberry sprinkles to add a crunch.

SERVINGS
14 pretzels
NUTRITIONAL DATA PER SERVING
68kcals, 4g protein, 5g fat, 3g carbs, 2g fiber

INGREDIENTS
1/2 cup vanilla whey protein powder

2 tablespoons coconut oil, melted

1/4 cup coconut flour

1/4 cup almond milk

1/2 bar (50g) dark chocolate

DIRECTIONS

1. Preheat oven to 325° F (around 160° C).

2. In a bowl, mix together everything but the chocolate until you get a sort of "dough" that can be flattened with a rolling pin.

3. Roll out the dough on a nonstick surface or parchment paper.

4. Using your pretzel cutter, cut out fourteen pretzels.

5. Bake the pretzels on a cookie sheet lined with parchment paper or silicone for about 10 minutes or until they're cooked through. You don't want to bake them to death—remove it before they brown; all they need is to cook through.

6. Melt your chocolate as described on page 141 and dip the pretzels in there one at a time.

7. Put them in the fridge for a couple of hours or the freezer for 30 minutes and BOOOOM! Ready. :-)

WHEN I MADE THESE, IT HAD BEEN YEARS SINCE I'D HAD A CINNAMON-SUGAR DONUT.

I had no idea. I just bit into these donuts and FWAAAAAA, I remembered being ten again! Memories are just so weird. They're weird because they hide behind pillars sometimes, and years can go by without you seeing them. You THINK you remember all there is to remember—as long as you sit back, close your eyes, and carefully retrace your steps. But no. There are things that only certain contexts bring to life: memories that only smells evoke, that particular feelings stir up, that specific situations awaken.

When I bit into these donuts, I felt like I was a kid again. It was all, "Mom! Mom! Can you get me one of those donuts?" Because, mmmm . . . the taste and subtle crunch of granulated sugar against a soft, moist, and perfectly cakey donut. I had totally forgotten about these donuts featuring in my childhood . . . until I took my first bite, and then the gates of nostalgia burst open and so many happy memories came pouring in.

CINNAMON "SUGAR" PROTEIN DONUTS

SERVINGS

8 donuts

NUTRITIONAL DATA PER SERVING

105.2kcals, 10g protein, 6.8g carbs, 3.55g fat, 2.3g fiber

INGREDIENTS

1/4 cup vanilla whey protein powder

1/4 cup vanilla pea protein powder

1 cup liquid egg whites

3 tablespoons cottage cheese (or ricotta)

1/4 cup coconut flour

1/2 cup coconut milk

1 teaspoon baking soda

1/4 cup date syrup

2 tablespoons granulated stevia

2 tablespoons cinnamon

DIRECTIONS

1. Preheat oven to 325°F (around 160°C).

2. Blend the protein powders with the egg whites, cottage cheese, coconut flour, coconut milk, and baking soda.

3. Pour the batter into a donut tray or muffin pan.

4. Bake for about 20 minutes, or until a knife inserted into the middle comes out clean. Watch out not to overbake them, because if you do, they'll be a bit dry.

5. Once baked, let them cool, remove them from the donut tray or muffin pan, and squeeze some date syrup on top of each donut.

6. Mix together the stevia and cinnamon. Sprinkle the donuts (or downright besiege them) with the stevia and cinnamon. Then, press and roll them in the stevia and cinnamon so that the cinnamon-y stevia sticks to the donuts.

DARK CHOCOLATE WHEY PROTEIN–COVERED WALNUTS

There are few things that I simply cannot resist, but moderation gets forcefully drop-kicked out the window when it comes to chocolate-covered nuts. There you lose me. Or rather, I lose myself. ;-)

Because the thing is, I LOVE dark chocolate–covered nuts. LOVE them. I can honestly sit there and munch dozens of them, going up the ladder of elation as I do without a care in the world. Okay, enough blah blah from me. Are you ready for the recipe? Because, I tell ya, these protein powder dark chocolate–covered nuts are a revoluuuuuuution!

SERVINGS

4 handfuls

NUTRITIONAL DATA PER SERVING

275kcals, 11g protein, 9g carbs, 25.6g fat, 4.5g fiber

INGREDIENTS

About 2/3 (60g) 100 percent dark chocolate bar, divided

1/4 cup chocolate whey protein powder

1 cup walnut halves

1 teaspoon cocoa powder

DIRECTIONS

1. Melt half of your dark chocolate as described on page 141.

2. When the chocolate has melted, throw in the protein powder and the walnuts and mix with a spoon.

3. Place the chocolate-covered walnuts on a cookie sheet lined with parchment paper or silicone (you want them separated from one another).

4. Then melt the rest of the chocolate and pour it over the nuts.

5. Sprinkle with cocoa (you can sprinkle with cinnamon, too, mmmmm).

6. Place the tray in the freezer for half an hour.

7. Separate into four equal-size servings.

DARK CHOCOLATE & PROTEIN–COVERED PUMPKIN SEEDS

My jaw dropped several feet when I tried these pumpkin seeds! And it's weird, because the protein powder has this bite to it that's hard to describe (it's almost crunchy but not really?), and this outer sweetness goes gorgeously well alongside the dark chocolate. And then! Then! Then you get to the pumpkin seeds and boooom, all the flavors come together in a truly spectacular fashion. :-D And you get so much goodness with every bite, as pumpkin seeds are rich in phytosterols, phosphorous, L-tryptophan, magnesium, zinc, iron, vitamin E, and vitamin K, and have tons of health benefits (while chocolate, in its darkest form, is brimming with antioxidants and polyphenols and—in moderation, of course—has also been linked to all kinds of health benefits).

SERVINGS
2 handfuls

NUTRITIONAL DATA PER SERVING
178.45kcals, 12.3g protein, 6g carbs, 13.2g fat, 2.5g fiber

INGREDIENTS
1/5 bar (20g) dark chocolate (ideally 85 percent or higher)
1/4 cup chocolate whey protein powder
1/4 cup pumpkin seeds

DIRECTIONS

1. Melt the chocolate as described on page 141.

2. Add the protein powder and pumpkin seeds to the melted chocolate, and mix with a spoon.

3. Spread out on a cookie sheet lined with parchment paper or silicone and chill in the fridge for about 30 minutes. That, dear members of the jury, is IT. :-D

IF YOU MAKE THESE, REMEMBER
TO USE DECAFFEINATED BEANS
IF YOU PLAN ON EATING A BUNCH
OF THEM (ESPECIALLY IN THE
LATE AFTERNOON OR EVENING!).
I MADE THE MISTAKE OF EATING
A HANDFUL ONE EVENING AND
MUST HAVE COUNTED THREE
MILLION SHEEP BEFORE I
FINALLY FELL ASLEEP.

CHOCOLATE-COVERED ESPRESSO BEANS

SERVINGS

2 handfuls

NUTRITIONAL DATA PER SERVING

151kcals, 20.8g protein, 8.35g carbs, 16.5g fat, 4.85g fiber

INGREDIENTS

3/4 bar (75g) dark chocolate (85 percent or higher)

1/4 cup chocolate whey protein powder

1/4 cup espresso beans

2 tablespoons cocoa powder

DIRECTIONS

1. Melt the chocolate as described on page 141.

2. Mix the protein powder into the melted chocolate and throw the espresso beans in there to coat them.

3. Roll the chocolate-and-protein-powder–covered espresso beans in the cocoa powder, place them on a cookie tray or silicone pan, and transfer them to the fridge for 30 minutes, so the chocolate can set. That's it!

STRAWBERRY- AND VANILLA-FILLED CHOCOLATE PROTEIN WHOOPEE PIES

SERVINGS

4 cakes

NUTRITIONAL DATA PER SERVING

248kcals, 30g protein, 28g carbs, 4g fat.

INGREDIENTS

CAKE LAYERS

1/2 cup liquid egg whites

1/2 cup chocolate pea protein powder

2 tablespoons cocoa powder

3 tablespoons xylitol

1/4 cup rolled oats (gluten-free or regular)

1/4 cup almond milk

1/2 teaspoon baking powder

CREAM FILLING

1/4 cup vanilla (or strawberry) whey protein powder

3/4 cup Greek yogurt

1-2 tablespoons strawberry (or vanilla) casein
    protein powder

DIRECTIONS

1. Preheat oven to 325˚ F (around 160˚ C).

2. Blend all ingredients for the cake layers together. Spoon four separate "cakes" onto a cookie sheet lined with parchment or silicone.

3. Bake for about 15 minutes or until a knife inserted into the middle comes out clean. Remove from oven and let cool.

4. Meanwhile, blend the filling ingredients together. Use more or less protein powder, depending on how thick you want your filling.

5. Slice the cooled cakes horizontally to make room for the filling. (You could also leave them whole for super thick whoopee pies.) Spread the filling thickly between the layers.

PROTEIN
CAKE &
PIES &
CHEESECAKES

DARK CHOCOLATE & ALMOND PROTEIN CHEESECAKE

Welcome, welcome to a recipe to die(t) for. This cheesecake is outstanding. And the macros, the macros! Check this out: each slice packs 10 grams of carbs, 9 grams of fat, and a whopping 30 grams of protein—kaPOW! It's as close to protein magic as one can get. I don't know how to begin describing it. It is just delicious. It's spectacular. Eating it was a spiritual moment for me. It was emotional. It was intense. And . . . I almost ate the plate.

SERVINGS
8 slices

NUTRITIONAL DATA PER SERVING
242kcals, 30g protein, 10g carbs, 9g fat

INGREDIENTS

BASE
2 tablespoons light tahini (or almond butter)
1/2 cup ground almonds
1 tablespoon agave syrup

FILLING
1 cup Greek yogurt
1 cup quark or low-fat ricotta cheese
1/4 cup vanilla whey protein powder
1/4 cup liquid egg whites

TOPPING
2/3 bar (60g) 85–95 percent dark chocolate

DIRECTIONS

1. Preheat oven to 325°F (around 160°C).

2. In a bowl, mix all base ingredients together. (You can replace the agave with honey or calorie-free syrup if you want the whole thing to be lower in carbs.) Once you have a crumbly mix, press it down into a small springform pan. If you want to use a medium or large pan, just double the amounts for the whole thing.

3. After that, blend all filling ingredients in a bowl.

4. Pour the cheesecake filling onto the base.

5. Bake for about 30–45 minutes. Now, this part is important: do not overbake your cheesecake. You want to remove it from the oven while it's still wobbly in the middle and feels undercooked. Don't let it cook all the way; you want it wet inside—it will set as it cools and stay creamy in the center. Trust me on this.

6. Let it cool, and, when you're ready to serve it, melt the chocolate according to the directions on page 141, and drizzle some on top of your individual slices!

EVER SINCE PROTEINPOW.COM WAS BORN, PEOPLE HAVE BEEN ASKING ME FOR A RECIPE FOR PROTEIN KEY LIME PIE.

I've gotten dozens of emails, messages, tweets, and Instagram requests about it. And I've resisted. For more than two years I've resisted. Not out of cruelty or a scheming desire to delay people's gratifications. No.

I've resisted simply because I don't like citrusy stuff. I've been like that for as long as I can remember—turning down lime-flavored Jello, saying no to lemon meringue pie, scrunching up my nose when in the vicinity of lemon juice, and powerfully recoiling from the very idea of a lemonade stand. I just didn't get the appeal.

But a few months ago, when we played our monthly Pick the Next Recipe Game on Facebook, I thought to include Protein Key Lime Pie as an option. Just out of curiosity, really—I wanted to gauge whether people were still as fervent about it as they had been in the past. And indeed they were! People who voted for me to make a Protein Key Lime Pie did so with great passion.

Someone, for example, didn't vote by just saying "Protein Key Lime Pie." No. She wrote: "Protein Key Lime Pie! Protein Key Lime Pie! Protein Key Lime Pie! Protein Key Lime Pie! Protein Key Lime Pie! Protein Key Lime Pie! Protein Key Lime Pie! Pleeeeeeeeease!!!!!!!!" And she wasn't alone. Someone else wrote, "Protein Key Lime Pie! Please! Please! Please!" And it went on and on. It was clear that people really wanted it.

How could I turn a blind eye to that?

So I decided to give Protein Key Lime Pie a chance. I put my citrus aversion to the side. And guess what? I LOVE IT. I'm eating my words (and the pie!) right now because it's sensational. It's citrusy yet perfectly sweet. At the same time, it's creamy and smooth and oh! I'm converted! Yes, it turned out a bit like a cheesecake, but sweet Mount Olympus! What a cheesecake! I can't wait for you to try it; you'll fall head over heels in love.

KEY LIME PROTEIN CHEESECAKE

SERVINGS

8 slices

NUTRITIONAL DATA PER SERVING

144kcals, 17g protein, 4g carbs, 7g fat, 2g fiber

INGREDIENTS

BASE

1/2 cup ground almonds

1 1/2 teaspoons toffee stevia

3 tablespoons almond milk (or coconut milk)

3 tablespoons light tahini (or peanut butter)

FILLING

1 1/4 cups Greek yogurt

1/2 cup vanilla whey protein powder

1/4 cup vanilla casein protein powder

2 eggs

2 teaspoons toffee stevia or your
     sweetener of choice

1 tablespoon key lime juice or flavoring

Zest of 1/2 lime

1 tablespoon vanilla extract

1 thinly sliced lime, for decoration (optional)

"WHIPPED CREAM"

3/4 cup Greek yogurt

1/4 cup vanilla casein
    protein powder

DIRECTIONS

1. Preheat oven to 375°F (around 190°C).

2. Mix the base ingredients together and press into a small springform pan. I used a 6-inch pan and pressed the mixture down using a soft-tipped silicone spatula, but you can use your fingers, too.

3. Stick that in the oven and bake it for 10 minutes.

4. Blend the filling ingredients together, except the sliced lime, and pour the mix onto the base.

5. Turn the heat down to 325°F (around 160°C).

6. Bake for about 45–55 minutes, or until when you shake it, it wobbles a bit in the center but not the sides. You want to remove it from the oven while it's still wobbly in the center. DO NOT let it cook through. In a way, we're pretty much making a cheesecake here!

7. As the filling cools, the center will set, and the whole thing will stay firm yet creamy.

8. Once it's all nicely cooled, make the "whipped cream" by mixing the yogurt and casein protein powder and sticking that in a piping bag with a nozzle at the end (or a plastic bag with the corner cut off), then adding a dollop to each slice.

9. Add some sliced lime or lime zest for further decoration if you like.

ONE OF THE BEST & EASIEST PROTEIN CHEESECAKES

This is a carnivore's protein cheesecake. That's right, I made it using vanilla-flavored beef protein powder. Now, if you don't have beef protein powder, don't worry: just use whey—it'll do the same job. For the crust, I used only one ingredient: almonds! It really doesn't need much else because the filling holds it together. You could add a nut butter to the ground almonds (along with some honey if you want your base to be firmer and less crunchy), but I really liked the simplicity of this recipe because you don't have to do anything to get the "crust"—you just pour the filling on top!

SERVINGS

8 slices

NUTRITIONAL DATA PER SERVING

89kcals, 9.37g protein, 3.25g carbs, 3.87g fat

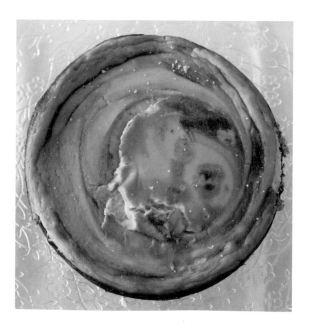

INGREDIENTS

3/4 cup ground almonds

1 1/4 cups quark, low-fat ricotta, mascarpone, or blended cottage cheese and Greek yogurt

1/4 cup vanilla-caramel beef protein powder (or vanilla whey protein powder)

1 egg

1 egg white

2 tablespoons coconut flour

2 tablespoons freshly brewed espresso

DIRECTIONS

1. Preheat oven to 350˚F (around 175˚C).

2. First, add the ground almonds to the bottom of a springform pan (I used a 6-inch one) and flatten them with a spoon.

3. Then blend your filling ingredients, except the espresso, using a handheld blender or food processor. You can add some sweetener if you want your cheesecake sweeter. (I didn't add any because I think it's fine without it, but listen to your taste buds on this one, okay?)

4. Once blended, pour it all on top of the ground almonds.

5. Add the espresso on top of the filling and move it around with a spoon to form some swirls. You could blend the espresso WITH the filling, but if you add it on top, it looks nice.

6. Finally, bake for about 35 minutes, or until your house smells like heaven and when you shake the cheesecake, it wiggles a bit in the center.

7. Once it gets to this point, remove it from the oven, and let it cool before you release it from the pan. Then, slice it, aaaaand . . . ENJOY!

MY DAD'S RASPBERRY PROTEIN CHEESECAKE

You don't know this, but my dad LOVES protein cheesecake. He's always asking me to upload protein cheesecake recipes on proteinpow.com, and, when I make them for him in person, he destroys them. So, this cheesecake is proudly dedicated to him. Here's to you, Pa! A recipe for quite possibly one of the best protein cheesecakes I've ever made. I think the egg white protein powder is the star here, adding an extra vanilla custard-ness while binding the whole thing together beautifully. The base is more like a cookie—crumbly, crunchy, and nommmmly complementing the creaminess on top. Oh, la, la, la! Please do try this. It's madness on a plate.

SERVINGS
8 slices

NUTRITIONAL DATA PER SERVING
189kcals, 13g protein, 11g carbs, 11g fat, 2.2g fiber

INGREDIENTS
BASE
1 3/4 cups ground or slivered almonds
2 pitted medjool dates
1 1/2 teaspoons sunflower seed butter (or peanut butter)
1 teaspoon wattleseeds (or 2 more pitted medjool dates)

FILLING
1 1/4 cups quark, Greek yogurt, low-fat ricotta, or mascarpone
3 tablespoons vanilla custard egg white protein powder
1 cup whole milk
5 tablespoons vanilla casein protein powder

TOPPING
1 cup fresh or frozen raspberries

DIRECTIONS
1. Preheat oven to 350°F (around 175°C).

2. Using an immersion blender, blender, or food processor, blend all base ingredients together.

3. Press the base mixture into a pie tin and bake for about 15 minutes.

4. Using an immersion blender, blender, or food processor, blend all filling ingredients together.

5. Take base out of the oven and leave to cool.

6. Once cooled, add the filling mixture on top, then the raspberries.

7. Bake for about 35–45 minutes. Keep an eye on it, and take it out as SOON as it feels taut when you press it lightly with your finger. You don't want to overbake it, because then you'll end up with a weird cousin of cheesecake that'll give you sadface, and we don't want THAT.

8. Let it cool and then cut yourself a slice.

THIS RECIPE CONTAINS EXPLICIT CONTENT AND GRAPHIC REFERENCES TO PROTEIN FORN:

protein forn | (\\'prō-tēin'forn\\ noun.

1. glamorized and provocative photographs of protein food.

2. the glorification of protein food in the context of arousing an excessive desire to eat it.

It all began like this:

"Oh yeah, baby!"

"Oh my God, that's amazing."

"Oh yes!"

"Ohhh . . ."

"Do it slowly, yeah, like that."

"Like this?"

"Yes . . . oh. . . . That's incredible!"

"Wow . . ."

"Hold it there, hold it . . . ohhhhh!"

"OH!"

Had the window to my house been open, my neighbors would most likely have closed theirs, full of indignation at the (literal) airing of my private affairs. The next day I would have gotten funny denunciatory looks, full of disapproval and . . . outrage.

Thankfully, however, the windows were closed.

But what was happening? You may be wondering. I'll tell you: my friend Will was pouring Crème du Cinnamon Roll on the cake, and I was taking pictures. That's it. It couldn't have been a more innocent act! And it culminated with us devouring the cake in a forn trance. Because, Zeus! It was spectacular—decadent, rich, moist, almost fudge-like, and oh! Luxurious! And the whole time we were going:

"This is crazy! How can this actually be healthy?!"

"Without sugar, flour, or simple carbs!"

"Without gluten!"

"This is madness!"

"Madness!"

CHOCOLATE PROTEIN CAKE WITH CRÈME DU CINNAMON ROLL (NC-17)

SERVINGS

5 cakes

NUTRITIONAL DATA PER SERVING

391kcals, 39g protein, 12g carbs, 20g fat, 3g fiber

INGREDIENTS

CAKE

1 1/2 cups yogurt

1 cup pea protein powder

1/2 cup chopped walnuts

1/4 cup cocoa powder

1 cup liquid egg whites

3 tablespoons plus 1 teaspoon coconut flour

2 tablespoons chopped cacao nibs

2 tablespoons vanilla-flavored stevia

CRÈME DU CINNAMON ROLL

1/4 cup cinnamon roll–flavored whey protein
powder, casein protein powder,
or a blend of the two

Water (or milk) to bind into a cream

DIRECTIONS

1. Preheat oven to 375°F (around 190°C).

2. Blend cake ingredients together, pour into cups of a muffin pan (I made 5), and bake for about 45 minutes, or until a knife inserted into the middle of one of the muffins comes out clean. That's it.

3. For the Crème du Cinnamon Roll, mix the cinnamon roll–flavored protein powder (it could be whey protein powder, casein protein powder, or a blend of the two) with water or milk until you get a syrupy consistency.

4. When ready to serve, pour the sauce over the cakes.

A FEW MONTHS AGO I WAS ON THE TRAIN—IT WAS 9:00 A.M., AND I WAS HEADING TO THE CITY OF SOUTHAMPTON, IN ENGLAND. ACROSS FROM ME WAS A WOMAN READING A NEWSPAPER.

Half an hour into the journey, I got hungry. I hadn't had breakfast, so . . . I opened my bag, pulled out a Tupperware, opened it, and proceeded to devour a gigantic slice of protein cake. The cake was made with blueberries, yogurt, rolled oats, protein powder, egg whites, and almonds. It was really big, creamy, tall, and to me, it constituted a pretty well-rounded breakfast.

But to this woman? Oh, no. To this woman, I was conducting an act of unspeakable gluttony—I was a heart attack waiting to happen. Either that or I was Bridget Jones–ing my way to a voluptuous new me.

Her eyes were full of outrage while I was eating it—à la how-could-you-be-eating-ALL-that-CAKE-at-9:30-a.m.! But there I was, smiling ear to ear—enjoying my creation with gusto.

I'm telling you this because the exact same thing happened the day I made the cake in this recipe, only this time it was at the gym. And this time, one could say the outrage was more intense (because the gym tends to make people more aware of their and others' food choices).

I had just finished my workout and I grabbed a free seat across from a woman who looked like she had just finished working out (all the tables are shared at the gym I go to because, well, there aren't that many). I opened my bag, took out my Tupperware, "exposed" a big slice of cake, and BOOM: I ate it!

The woman gave me a look of "Are you sure that's the best thing to be eating post-workout?" The kind of look that you and I probably save for the people who down all kinds of junk food after the gym because they've "earned it." Ha! Little did she know that this cake was, in fact, full of nutritious goodness!

MY POST-WORKOUT CHOCOLATE PROTEIN CAKE

SERVINGS

8 slices

NUTRITIONAL DATA PER SERVING

155.2kcals, 12.5g protein, 19g carbs, 2.5g fat, 5g fiber

INGREDIENTS

1 1/4 cups cooked aduki (or black) beans, rinsed and drained

1/2 cup liquid egg whites

1/2 cup chocolate whey protein powder

1 1/4 cups low-fat cottage cheese

1/2 cup cocoa powder, plus more for sprinkling on top

6 tablespoons date syrup

3 tablespoons coconut flour

1 teaspoon baking powder

DIRECTIONS

1. Preheat oven to 350˚F (around 170˚C).

2. Using an immersion blender, blender, or food processor, blend all ingredients together and place in a cake pan.

3. Bake for about 40–45 minutes, or until a knife inserted into the middle comes out clean. Make sure you don't overbake the cake. You want it JUST cooked, ideally still a bit gooey in the center, so it's nice and moist inside. :-)

4. When it's done, let it cool, take it out of the pan, and sprinkle some cocoa on top!

COFFEE & DARK CHOCOLATE PROTEIN CAKE TOWER

This recipe is for a protein cake tower that combines two of the tastiest foods on earth: coffee and dark chocolate. As a result, the end product is really yummy. I loved it, and, if you like coffee and chocolate as much as I do, I think you'll love it, too! Part of why this cake is so cool is that it's low in carbs yet doesn't seem like it at all. I mean, it tastes like a regular butter-flour-sugar-chocolate-and-coffee cake. But . . . it isn't. It's packed full of protein, instead.

SERVINGS

8 slices

NUTRITIONAL DATA PER SERVING

158kcals, 12.4g protein, 4.8g carbs, 8.8g fat, 2.4g fiber

INGREDIENTS

CAKE

1/2 cup liquid egg whites

1/4 cup plus 1 tablespoon coconut flour

1/2 cup chocolate vegan protein powder (it could be chocolate pea protein powder, chocolate rice protein powder, chocolate hemp protein powder, or a blend of two or all of them)

1 tablespoon instant coffee powder

1/4 cup acai berry powder

2 tablespoons cocoa powder

1 1/2 cups coconut milk (or any other milk)

1/2 teaspoon baking powder

FROSTING

1/4 cup vanilla vegan protein powder (again, could be chocolate pea protein powder, chocolate rice protein powder, chocolate hemp protein powder, or a blend of two or all of them)

1 teaspoon vanilla extract

1/4 cup freshly brewed espresso

Water to bind

Cocoa and/or pomegranate seeds, optional

DIRECTIONS

1. Preheat oven to 325°F (around 160°C).

2. Using an immersion blender, blender, or food processor, blend all cake ingredients together.

3. Place batter in a loaf pan and bake for 40–45 minutes, or until a knife inserted into the middle comes out clean.

4. Once the cake is done, allow it to cool and slice it in half so you end up with two squares. Then slice each square horizontally, so you end up with four layers.

5. Place all frosting ingredients except the cocoa and pomegranates in a bowl and mix until consistently smooth.

6. Spread the frosting between the layers of cake, add some cocoa, and, if you want, you can add some pomegranate seeds on top. You don't have to—they're just there for color—but if you want them, go for it.

WHEY PROTEIN COFFEE CAKE

Coffee cake has simply got to be one of the best cakes ever. I mean, it combines two of the greatest things on earth: coffee (a.k.a. the nectar of the gods) and cake! And when you power it up with protein and then dip it in more coffee? Well, well, well! It's a pre-workout snack of Olympian proportions! Just remember not to dunk the cake too long inside your coffee. I like to dip it in for five or ten seconds, so it absorbs as much of the coffee as it can without disintegrating. There's nothing worse than lifting your cake out of the coffee and realizing it's gone (it reminds me of the girl who was recording a YouTube tutorial on using hair curlers and accidentally burnt off her hair by leaving the curler wrapped around her hair for too long!). It's like, "Yay! Things are going great here! Look at how I'm bossing this! So easy! So cool!" and then . . . BAM! Disaster. We don't want that.

SERVINGS
8 cake bars

NUTRITIONAL DATA PER SERVING
86kcals, 10g protein, 5.2g carbs, 1.8g fat, 2.4g fiber

INGREDIENTS
1/2 cup rolled oats (gluten-free or regular)

3 1/2 teaspoons coconut flour

1/2 cup vanilla whey protein powder (or, if you have coffee-flavored whey protein powder, use that)

1 1/2 cups liquid egg whites

1/2 shot freshly made espresso

1 tablespoon instant coffee powder

1 teaspoon baking powder

DIRECTIONS
1. Preheat oven to 325°F (around 160°C).

2. Using an immersion blender, blender, or food processor, blend all ingredients together.

3. Place mixture in a mini loaf pan and bake for 35–40 minutes, or until a knife inserted into the middle comes out clean.

4. Remove from the pan and leave to cool.

5. Once it cools, cut it into eight bars, and then make yourself a fresh cup of joe. Dip the cake in there and enjoy.

VANILLA-CARAMEL PROTEIN COFFEE CAKE

If you were to join me for a cup of coffee, I'd probably order a double espresso, a traditional macchiato, a black Americano, or just a cup of black tea along with a single shot of espresso. I'd probably pause and examine the menu before ordering, though, and go through the lattes, the mochas, the cappuccinos, the seasonal drinks, and the breves (which are so delicious but unfortunately also a calorific assault to the system, boooo). Ah, there are just so many different kinds of espresso-based drinks! And so many different flavor combinations! This cake right here is a tribute to one of the tastiest coffee drinks I've ever had. I tried it in a coffee shop in downtown Chicago a few years back, and, I swear, it made me wonder whether the barista was human or divine . . .

What's the cake like? It's like a vanilla and caramel macchiato! Absolutely celestial. It reminds me of a tiramisu, but it's more caramel-y, more vanilla-y, and coffee-cakey. Oh! It's delicious—try it. What's most shocking about it is how soft and fluffy the cake is, particularly when you bear in mind its crazy macros!

SERVINGS
2 small cakes

NUTRITIONAL DATA PER SERVING
142.6kcals, 24.6g protein, 6.4g carbs, 1.1g fat, 2.7g fiber

INGREDIENTS
CAKE
1/2 cup liquid egg whites

1/2 cup vanilla brown rice protein powder

2 tablespoons vanilla brown rice protein powder

1 double espresso

3/4 cup quark (or low-fat ricotta or mascarpone)

2 tablespoons coconut flour

1 tablespoon vanilla extract

1 teaspoon baking powder

FROSTING
3/4 cup quark (or low-fat ricotta or mascarpone)

1 tablespoon vanilla casein protein powder

1 tablespoon toffee flavdrops or your sweetener of choice

DIRECTIONS
1. Preheat oven to 350°F (around 175°C).

2. Using an immersion blender, blender, or food processor, blend all cake ingredients together.

3. Place mixture in two silicone mini loaf pans or muffin tins and bake for 30 minutes, or until a knife inserted into the middle comes out clean.

4. To make the frosting, mix the quark with the vanilla casein protein powder and toffee flavdrops (or your sweetener of choice).

5. Trim the edges of the cakes and slice the cakes in half horizontally.

6. Once the cakes have cooled, spread the frosting on two halves and top with the other two halves.

ORGANIC WHEY PROTEIN GLUTEN-FREE CARROT CAKE

I baked this cake in a loaf pan because I wanted to slice it into bread slices, but feel free to bake it in a round cake pan if you want to end up with nice triangular slices of cake. The final product was great, especially topped with cream cheese and/or almond butter!

SERVINGS
1 cake
NUTRITIONAL DATA PER 1/10 CAKE
68.7kcals, 6.6g protein, 7g carbs, 1.2g fat, 2.2g fiber

INGREDIENTS

3/4 cup liquid egg whites
1/2 cup organic vanilla whey protein powder
1 banana
1/2 cup quinoa flakes (or millet flakes, buckwheat flakes, or rolled oats)
2 tablespoons coconut flour
1 teaspoon baking powder
1 tablespoon vanilla extract
1 tablespoon cinnamon
1 tablespoon toffee stevia or your sweetener of choice
1/4 cup peeled and grated carrot
Almond butter, cream cheese, or butter for
     topping (optional)

DIRECTIONS

1. Preheat oven to 325˚F (around 160˚C).

2. Using an immersion blender, blender, or food processor, blend all ingredients together, except the carrot.

3. Stir the carrot into the above blended mixture (you don't want to blend the carrot in the mix because you want it to retain its crunchy texture).

4. Place batter in a loaf pan and bake for 35–40 minutes, or until a knife inserted into the middle comes out clean.

5. Remove from the oven and leave to cool.

6. Top with some almond butter, cream cheese, or grass-fed butter. This is optional, of course, but absolutely lovely!

DARK CHOCOLATE PROTEIN TARTLETS

I made these tartlets as a tribute to dark chocolate because, I don't know about you, but I love eating dark chocolate. I eat it every day. If you're thinking, "Oh, Anna, that's not a good habit to have! Chocolate isn't that good for you!" You're wrong. Chocolate is great! Well, dark chocolate is. It's a powerful source of antioxidants and has a host of health benefits. Did I mention that it's also the most delicious thing on earth? Because it is. To me, at least!

SERVINGS

2 tartlets

NUTRITIONAL DATA PER SERVING

256.5kcals, 32g protein, 21.7g carbs, 4.5g fat, 2.85g fiber

INGREDIENTS

BASE

1/4 cup chocolate pea protein powder
1/2 cup liquid egg whites
1 tablespoon date syrup
1/2 cup rolled oats (gluten-free or regular)
1/4 cup coconut milk
1 1/2 teaspoons coconut flour

FILLING

2 tablespoons chocolate pea protein powder
2 tablespoons cocoa powder
1 tablespoon date syrup
1/2 cup liquid egg whites

TOPPING

2 tablespoons cocoa powder

DIRECTIONS

1. Preheat oven to 375°F (around 190°C).

2. Mix all your base ingredients together using a spoon, until a thick sort of dough is formed.

3. Get two mini tart pans out and split the base dough between them, pressing it down with a spoon so as to cover the bottom and sides of each pan.

4. Stick the bases in the oven and remove them as soon as they brown. It won't take long—around 10 minutes—so keep an eye on them.

5. Allow them to cool. Meanwhile, make the filling by mixing all the filling ingredients together in a bowl.

6. Top each base with half the mixture (you don't need to bake them again; the filling is "raw").

7. Once both the tartlets are prepared, sprinkle cocoa powder on top.

8. Finally, transfer the tartlets to the fridge to allow the filling to set a bit.

DARK CHOCOLATE PROTEIN PIE WITH PECANS

When I created this recipe, my goal was to create a Protein Chocolate Pecan Pie. But, instead, what I ended up with was a Dark Chocolate Protein Pie with Pecans! I think for it to have been more pecan pie-ish, a whole bunch of vanilla needed to have been mobilized, and some kind of golden-syrupy and cinnamon-ish uhmph factor. That being said, what a pie this was! I was super happy with the result, particularly with the way the base fused with the mmmm chocolate filling.

SERVINGS
8 slices

NUTRITIONAL DATA PER SERVING
173kcals, 12.6g protein, 15g carbs, 7.4g fat, 4g fiber

INGREDIENTS

BASE
3 big apples, cored and chopped (approximately 1 1/4 cups)
1/2 cup quinoa flakes (or rolled oats or buckwheat flakes)
2 tablespoons butter (or coconut oil if you're not a fan of butter)
2 tablespoons buckwheat flakes (or rolled oats)
1 egg
1/4 cup vanilla whey protein powder
1 tablespoon chocolate or vanilla brown rice protein powder

FILLING
8 egg whites
1/4 cup chocolate hemp protein powder
2 tablespoons psyllium husks
2 tablespoons cocoa powder
1/4 cup pea protein powder
3 fat medjool dates (pitted)
1/4 cup whole pecans, for topping

DIRECTIONS

1. Preheat oven to 325˚F (around 160˚C).

2. Blend your apples with the rest of the ingredients for the base and add this mix to a pie mold.

3. Bake the base for 10–15 minutes, or until it looks and feels cooked.

4. Meanwhile, make your filling by blending together the filling ingredients, except the pecans.

5. Add the filling to the cooked base and top with pecans.

6. Bake at the same temperature for an additional 15–20 minutes, or until the top has cooked through.

I MADE THIS RECIPE USING TWO SMALL PIE MOLDS.

You can triple or even quadruple the ingredients to make a traditional-size pie, though (just make sure you adapt your cooking times). I made two small pies because I think small food is fun. It always reminds me of the standup skit where Jerry Seinfeld talks about using miniature soap in hotel rooms and feeling immensely muscular.

That's kind of how it is here: you cut yourself a slice of pie, and suddenly you can't help but think, "What if this slice of pie was regular size, and I was a giant eating it?"

Wrong.

Being a giant wouldn't be that much fun. In fact, it'd be very difficult. Finding clothes and furniture would be impossible, people would stare and whisper, you'd be forced to fight crime against your will, and you'd perpetually find yourself labeled as . . . "that giant."

Anyway, I digress. The point I was trying to make before I pulled out the violins is that small food can be fun! And it's also great if you have issues with portion control, as you can obliterate an entire pie and still have room for a cup of tea.

A FRIENDLY GIANT'S SWEET POTATO PROTEIN PIE

SERVINGS
2 mini pies

NUTRITIONAL DATA PER SERVING
444.5kcals, 32.2g protein, 39.9g carbs, 16.65g fat,
7.95g fiber

INGREDIENTS

CRUST
1/4 cup cashew nuts, chopped
1/2 cup rolled oats (gluten-free or regular)
1/4 cup vanilla pea, rice, or other veggie powder
2 tablespoons calorie-free maple syrup
    or date syrup
1/4 cup coconut milk (or almond milk or
    just regular cow's milk)

FILLING
1 medium sweet potato, peeled and cooked
    (boiled or baked)
1 tablespoon coconut flour
1/4 cup vanilla, caramel, or toffee
    whey protein powder
1 egg

DIRECTIONS

1. Preheat oven to 375˚F (around 190˚C).

2. Blend all the crust ingredients together, ideally using a food processor. You want to end up with a pasty kind of dough.

3. Press the dough into two small pie tins or one medium. If you don't have ANY pie tins, consider making this in muffin cups!

4. Once all the dough is in the pie tins, stick them in the oven and bake for about 15 minutes, or until they're slightly brown.

5. Meanwhile, to make the filling, blend the sweet potato with the coconut flour, protein powder and egg.

6. When the crusts are done, lower the oven temp to 325˚F (around 160˚C). Add the filling to the crusts.

7. Bake the pies at 325˚F for about 30–35 minutes, or until the filling has cooked through on top but not throughout. You don't want to totally cook the sweet potato filling, because the goal is for it to be creamy—pie-like, you know? You're not making a cake here.

8. Take the pies out of the oven as soon as they're cooked through inside and become kind of . . . custardy.

9. Let them set in the fridge for an hour before serving.

A DARK CHOCOLATE PRUNE-CONTAINING PROTEIN CAKE

I took it upon myself to make something delicious out of prunes. Could it be done? I wasn't sure. Could prunes be turned into something not only tasty but finger-lickingly luscious? Welcome to this recipe.

Oh! The melted heart! Oh, I was transported into another dimension, one with chocolate clouds and prunes holding onto magic wands. What a sensation! Let me try to explain why . . . the prunes in the cake give it this gorgeous kind of almost sticky texture (kind of like the British sticky toffee pudding?). Notice that here, other than coconut flour (which is, by nature, a heavy and dense flour), I'm not using any other texturizing "flour" (e.g., oats or buckwheat). It is the prunes, with the coconut flour, that—BOOOM!—give this cake its amazing, light, moist, and cakey consistency. Oh la la . . . What I did was eat half of one of the cakes post-workout (after licking the bowl thoroughly, because the batter was surreal and who could resist? Certainly not I) and then add a dollop of whipped cream to the other half.

SERVINGS

3 mini cakes

NUTRITIONAL DATA PER SERVING

326.1kcals, 28.1g protein, 29.8g carbs, 10.1g fat, 8.4g fiber

INGREDIENTS

1 cup liquid egg whites

1/2 cup dried prunes

1/2 cup cocoa powder

1/2 cup chocolate whey protein powder

1/2 cup coconut milk

3 tablespoons coconut flour

About 1/3 bar (30g) dark chocolate, broken into 3 squares

DIRECTIONS

1. Preheat your oven to 325˚F (around 160˚C).

2. Using an immersion blender, blender, or food processor, blend all ingredients except the chocolate.

3. Bake the mixture in a small cake pan or a couple of giant muffin tins for 35–40 minutes, or until a knife inserted into the middle comes out clean.

4. As soon as you take your cake or cakes out of the oven, insert a small square of dark chocolate inside and stick it or them back in the (turned off) oven for 5–10 minutes.

5. After 10 minutes, dig in!

A HEALTHY HIGH-PROTEIN APPLE CRUMBLE

This is probably one of my top ten protein pow(d)ered recipes. I love this apple crumble. LOVE it. I love its extreme simplicity, its flavor, its texture. I love its hefty punch of protein kaPOW! and the fact that it's gluten-free, sugar free, and nom, nom, nom—delicious!

SERVINGS

2 bowls

NUTRITIONAL DATA PER SERVING

310kcals, 33g protein, 16g carbs, 13g fat, 5g fiber

INGREDIENTS

1 1/4 cups quark, low-fat ricotta, or mascarpone

1/4 cup vanilla whey protein powder

2 small apples or 1 medium apple

1 tablespoon coconut flakes

1/2 teaspoon allspice

1/2 teaspoon cinnamon

1/2 teaspoon shaved vanilla beans

1/4 cup ground almonds

1 tablespoon slivered almonds

Cinnamon for topping

DIRECTIONS

1. Mix the quark (or low-fat ricotta or mascarpone) with the protein powder until you get a creamy pudding-type mixture (you COULD add a couple of drops of apple flavoring to this if you like extreme apple-ness). Put the mixture in a Tupperware and stick it in the freezer for an hour, or longer if you want more of an ice cream. :-)

2. Meanwhile, peel, slice, and steam the apple(s). You COULD leave the skin on, especially if you want the extra texture. I just always think that apple pie and apple crumble are best with peeled apples. If you're feeling lazy, though, don't peel it. It'll taste just as good.

3. To make the crumble topping, fry the coconut, spices, vanilla beans, and almonds at high heat in a dry nonstick pan. Mix them around with a wooden spoon so they don't burn. You basically just want them to brown a little and toast up. :-)

4. Divide the apples into two bowls and add half the quark-and-protein-powder mixture, then half the crumble mixture, then the rest of the dairy and protein-based mixture, and, finally, the second half of the crumble mixture.

5. Top the whole thing with cinnamon.

6. Devour!

THIS PIE ALMOST DIDN'T HAPPEN.
IT ALMOST DIDN'T MAKE IT.

It was close . . . close to being aggressively drop-kicked into the trash by my right Vibram. You might be thinking, "Whoa, woman, chill out! What happened?" Well, let me tell you. It all began quite innocently.

I woke up with a deep-seated desire to make a protein pie. The plan was simple: make a protein crust, bake it, pour the filling on it, and leave the whole thing to set in the fridge overnight. What could go wrong, right?

Well . . . a lot could go wrong.

Because what actually happened was this:

I went into my kitchen, made my protein crust, made the pie filling, and poured the filling into the crust—without baking the crust.

It took me a while to realize the error of my ways. And it looked horrendous. It was basically a raw crust with a gelatin filling on it—a filling that wasn't meant to be baked.

"Ack!" I thought. "What the Moses do I do now?!" Because there was no way I could leave it like it was.

The way I saw it, I had two options: a simple one and a messy one. The simple one involved me throwing the whole thing out and getting the hell out of the kitchen.

The messy one was a bit more complicated. It involved me dumping the filling out of the raw crust, baking the crust, making a new filling, and pouring the new filling onto the (this time) cooked crust.

I stood there looking at it for a while, unsure of which option to go with, because, quite frankly, I was pretty annoyed and ready to do something else with my time.

But I didn't want to give up on the whole thing. I felt a sense of responsibility toward those berries. I had, after all, personally picked them the day before!

So . . . I chose option two.

I poured out the filling, baked the crust, and made another filling. When the crust was cooked, I then added the new filling to it and allowed the whole thing to set in the fridge overnight as I had originally planned.

I didn't know what to expect when I cut into the pie the next day. I thought it could go either way. But guess what? It was splendid. Gorgeous. Delicious. Sublime. Ma-ha-ha-ha-gical! Here's the recipe.

BLACKBERRY PROTEIN PIE

SERVINGS

8 slices

NUTRITIONAL DATA PER SERVING

104kcals, 11g protein, 6g carbs, 4g fat, 4g fiber

INGREDIENTS

BASE

3/4 cup vanilla pea protein powder

2 tablespoons sweetener (I used a vanilla-flavored one, but any will do)

2 tablespoons pumpkin seed butter (or sunflower seed butter)

3/4 cup almond milk

1 egg

FILLING

1 cup water

2 tablespoons powdered gelatin

1/4 cup powdered berry-flavored BCAAs (branched-chain amino acids)

1 cup fresh blackberries

DIRECTIONS

1. Preheat oven to 350˚F (around 175˚C).

2. Mix together base ingredients and press the mixture into the bottom and sides of a medium-size springform pan.

3. Bake for about 35–40 minutes, or until it looks and feels cooked.

4. Meanwhile, to make your filling, boil the water, add the gelatin to it, and mix until the gelatin has dissolved.

5. Take it off the heat, add the BCAAs, and then whisk the liquid until everything has mixed.

6. Add the fresh berries to the BCAA mix, and pour the mixture onto the cooked crust.

7. Leave the whole thing to set in the fridge overnight, and . . . voilà! Your very own homemade Blackberry Protein Pie.

THIS RECIPE INVOLVES FOUR EASY STEPS AND TAKES 13 MINUTES TO BAKE, 5 MINUTES TO ASSEMBLE, AND A LIFETIME TO ENJOY—BECAUSE, TRUST ME, YOU'LL MAKE THIS OVER AND OVER AGAIN!

Step one: Make a super fluffy and incredibly airy protein brownie cake (recipe on the next page).

Step two: Soak the brownies in espresso (oh yeah!).

Step three: Make a vanilla protein cream and top the soaked brownies.

Step four: Sprinkle the whole thing with cocoa powder: BOOM, done.

If you're thinking, "Oh, right, the brownies and the cream are probably hard to make," you're wrong. Even a toddler could master this (and I don't mean one of those gifted-in-the-kitchen toddlers, just a regular one).

The result is magnificently reminiscent of proper tiramisu and almost made me want to cry. Could it be any easier and quicker to make? Could it be any tastier? Zeus . . . and it's the brownies that made this so gorgeous; they're super airy and light, so they absorb all the espresso, creating this wonderfully moist pot of sweet chocolatey coffee heaven. Unbelievable . . . you guys have to try it; I don't know what else to say . . .

PROTEIN TIRAMISU

SERVINGS

3 small pots

NUTRITIONAL DATA PER SERVING

195kcals, 30g protein, 7g carbs, 3.8g fat, 2.6g fiber

INGREDIENTS

CAKE

1 cup liquid egg whites

1 cup mascarpone or ricotta cheese

1/2 cup chocolate whey protein powder

2 tablespoons cocoa powder

6 tablespoons coconut flour

1 teaspoon baking powder

TOPPING

1 1/2 shots espresso

1/4 cup quark or ricotta or mascarpone

1/4 cup vanilla or caramel whey protein powder

Cocoa for topping

DIRECTIONS

1. Preheat oven to 350°F (around 175°C).

2. Whisk together cake ingredients with a hand mixer for 3–5 minutes to give the egg whites a bit of body. Pour batter into a square cake pan (ideally silicone or else lined with parchment and greased) and bake for 12–15 minutes, or until a knife inserted into the middle comes out clean.

3. When the cake is ready, slice it into small squares.

4. To then transform the cake into tiramisu, get some of the squares of your chocolate cake and press them into three little glass bowls or ramekins.

5. Pour half a shot of the espresso on top of the cake.

6. While the cake absorbs all the coffee you poured on it, make the protein cream by mixing the quark (or ricotta or mascarpone) with the vanilla or caramel protein powder.

7. Top the espresso-infused cake with the vanilla cream and finish the whole thing off by sprinkling some cocoa on top.

8. You can proceed to violently devour one of the bowls, OR you can let it sit in the fridge for a couple of hours to allow the whole thing to set.

PROTEIN PUDDING FLUFF ICE-CREAN

LOW-FAT VANILLA & BANANA PROTEIN ICE CREAM

When people who have never cooked with their protein powders ask me what they should try making first, I always tell them to make protein ice cream and/or protein fluff.

They're the two easiest things to make with powders, and it's pretty hard to get them wrong, as they require no special skills, very few ingredients, and nothing other than a freezer, an immersion blender or food processor, and a bowl. Protein ice cream is also one of the best things to chase a grueling workout with, especially on a hot day!

SERVINGS

1 bowl

NUTRITIONAL DATA PER SERVING

217kcals, 31g protein, 24g carbs, 1g fat, 3g fiber

INGREDIENTS

1/4 cup low-fat cottage cheese
1/4 cup vanilla casein protein powder
1 banana, sliced and frozen

DIRECTIONS

1. Blend everything with an immersion blender or food processor.

2. Once it's all looking smooth and creamy, place in the freezer.

3. Every 30 minutes, remove from freezer, mix it around with a fork, and return it to freezer.

4. Repeat step 3 at least three times. By the fourth it should be thick—like ice cream—and be ready to be eaten!

MADAGASCAN BOURBON VANILLA PROTEIN ICE CREAM

Vanilla ice cream is one of my all-time favorites; it's simple, yes, but when made well, it's hard to beat. I made this one using actual Madagascan vanilla pods and some mascarpone, and it was lush: creamy, smooth, and absolutely heavenly! Why did I use mascarpone? Because it adds an extra creamy dimension to the ice cream (and tastes amazing when combined with sweet vanilla!).

SERVINGS
2 bowls

NUTRITIONAL DATA PER SERVING
261.1kcals, 36g protein, 11.5g carbs, 7.3g fat, 0.1g fiber

INGREDIENTS

3/4 cup quark (or low-fat ricotta or low-fat cream cheese)

1 tablespoon low-fat mascarpone cheese (or, again, ricotta)

1/2 cup vanilla whey protein powder

1 1/2 teaspoons vanilla flavoring powder

2 teaspoons Madagascan bourbon vanilla

DIRECTIONS

1. Blend all ingredients together with an immersion blender, blender, or food processor.

2. Once it's all looking smooth—like ice cream—place in freezer.

3. Every 30 minutes, remove from freezer, mix it around with a fork, and return it to freezer.

4. Repeat step 3 at least three times. By the fourth it should be thick—like ice cream!

5. Enjoy!

FIRST-TIME PROTEIN FLUFF

There's nothing like protein fluff! Whenever I describe it to people, I'm like a rabbit on speed, jumping up and down with the sheer delight that comes from knowing that soon their protein lives will change . . . forevah. And they do, much like yours will after you've tried this!

SERVINGS

1 bowl

NUTRITIONAL DATA PER SERVING

442kcals, 64g protein, 33g carbs, 6g fat, 8g fiber

INGREDIENTS

1/4 cup vanilla whey protein powder

2 cups frozen berries (I use a mixture)

1/4 cup milk

DIRECTIONS

1. First, blend everything together with a blender or food processor until smooth—sort of ice cream texture.

2. Then arm yourself with an electric hand mixer (unless you're Flash Gordon, you can't whisk it by hand) and whisk for 4–5 minutes, until you start to see mad gains in the mixture—the color will get lighter as the fluff gathers air under its wings and turns into real protein fluff.

3. That's it! You're done. Grab a spoon and dig in.

PROTEIN FLUFF

BLACKBERRY PROTEIN FLUFF

It's a question I get a lot: "Anna, what IS protein FLUFF?" If you've never had it, it's actually hard to describe. "Protein fluff is like . . . cloud!" I always say. "It's like eating light, airy, and fluffy heaven!" I get really excited when I describe it, to the point where people who've never tried it look at me like some sort of fluff-obsessed maniac. "What could POSSIBLY be THAT good?!" they wonder. Well, I'll tell you what: FLUFF.

SERVINGS
1 bowl

NUTRITIONAL DATA PER SERVING
204.6kcals, 29.3g protein, 19.9g carbs, 2g fat, 7g fiber

INGREDIENTS
1 cup frozen blackberries

1/4 cup vanilla or berry-flavored whey protein powder

2 tablespoons milk (I use coconut milk, but cow's milk does the job, too)

1 teaspoon vanilla stevia (this is optional but UNGH! Delicious!)

DIRECTIONS
1. Chuck everything in a bowl, and, using an immersion blender or regular blender, blend it together.

2. Once it's all looking smooth—like ice cream—whisk with an electric mixer for 4–5 minutes. This is where the magic happens, as your mixture starts to gain crazy volume and fluff up.

3. The final step is just to get a spoon out and dig into absolute protein deliciousness!

BANANA & PAPAYA PROTEIN FLUFF

Oh, protein fluff! You never cease to impress. I made this fluff by slicing and freezing some banana and papaya, and adding some spices, vanilla extract, and almond extract to the mix before freezing it in all in a Ziploc bag. Here's the recipe.

SERVINGS
1 bowl
NUTRITIONAL DATA PER SERVING
372kcals, 42g protein, 36.9g carbs, 7.1g fat, 5.4g fiber

INGREDIENTS

1 frozen sliced banana

1/2 cup frozen sliced papaya

1/2 teaspoon cinnamon

1/2 teaspoon vanilla extract

1/2 teaspoon almond extract (this is optional; it worked well, but it might have been better without it)

2 tablespoons to 1/4 cup milk

1/4 cup vanilla whey protein powder

DIRECTIONS

1. Put the fruit in a Ziploc bag and add the cinnamon, vanilla extract, and almond extract before sticking it in the freezer.

2. Once it is super frozen, use an immersion blender, blender, or food processor to blend all ingredients together until an ice cream–like mix is formed.

3. Using the whisker "head" part of an immersion blender, whisk the mix for a good 5 minutes. At first it wasn't fluffing that much my first time, but after minute three? Waaaaaa!!! It began to gain crazy volume and groooow.

VANILLA-TOFFEE SWEET POTATO PROTEIN FLUFF

Here's another fluff recipe! This time featuring, not fruit, but the almighty sweet potato!

SERVINGS

1 bowl

NUTRITIONAL DATA PER SERVING

253.7kcals, 26.5g protein, 30g carbs, 3.4g fat, 4.2g fiber

INGREDIENTS

1 medium sweet potato, cooked and FROZEN

1/2 cup vanilla whey protein powder

2 tablespoons milk

1 tablespoon toffee stevia or your sweetener of choice

1 teaspoon cinnamon for topping

DIRECTIONS

1. Blend together everything except the cinnamon until you get a smooth sort of ice cream texture.

2. Then, using an electric hand mixer, whisk everything together for 3–5 minutes, until the fluff has gained volume.

3. Then top it all with some cinnamon and enjoy!

COCONUT, CINNAMON & BANANA PROTEIN FLUFF

I've come to really like the idea of freezing fruit with different kinds of extracts. Here, I sliced a banana and added a tablespoon of coconut extract to the bag in which I froze the banana. When ready to fluff, I just blended the banana with almond milk and vanilla protein pow. Result? Amaazing! Especially topped with cinnamon and (mmm) pecans!

SERVINGS

1 bowl

NUTRITIONAL DATA PER SERVING

268.7kcals, 29.7g protein, 29.4g carbs, 4.4g fat

INGREDIENTS

1 banana, sliced and frozen

1 tablespoon coconut extract

2 tablespoons milk (I used almond but any will do)

1/4 cup vanilla whey protein powder

2 tablespoons pecans, chopped, for topping

1 teaspoon cinnamon for topping

DIRECTIONS

1. Freeze the sliced banana in a Ziploc bag with the coconut extract.

2. When frozen, blend with the milk until it forms a mush or sort of soft ice cream.

3. Then add the protein powder and whisk with an electric mixer for 5 minutes.

4. Add the nuts and cinnamon on top (this is optional but really nice!).

STRAWBERRY PROTEIN FLUFF

Protein fluff is just phenomenal. It takes no time. You can top it with nuts, use it to top protein jelly, have it on cake, have it IN cake, have it solo, have it inside a (protein?) cone, use it to top (protein?) pancakes, use it to top muffins—oh, any and every way! The stuff is grand. What's not to love about it?

SERVINGS

1 bowl

NUTRITIONAL DATA PER SERVING

442kcals, 64g protein, 33g carbs, 6g fat, 8g fiber

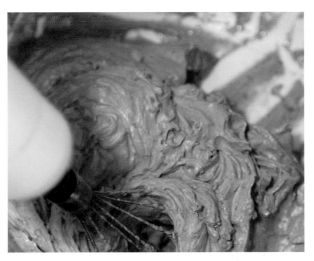

INGREDIENTS

1/4 cup vanilla or strawberry whey protein powder

1 cup frozen strawberries

2 tablespoons whole milk

1 teaspoon xanthan gum

DIRECTIONS

1. Blend all above ingredients together in a blender or food processor for a couple of minutes, until the mixture gets nice and ice-cream-y.

2. Then whisk it with the whisker head of an immersion blender or a hand or stand mixer for 5–8 minutes, until it gains volume and becomes fluff!

MY GRANDMA MAKES THE BEST RICE PUDDING IN THE WORLD.

It's creamy, sweet, perfectly balanced, and when served warm, well . . . it's disarming! It makes me want to cry. This recipe is a protein version of her famous pudding, and it's d-e-l-i-c-i-o-u-s. Mine is a bit different from my grandma's in that hers is made with sugar, and she uses a bit of cornstarch. She also uses whole cow's milk, whereas I prefer to use coconut milk or almond milk. Also, as you may have suspected, hers doesn't have protein powder. ;-) Taste-wise, though, they're comparable, and, Zeus, am I proud to say that! Because in the land of rice pudding, there just ain't no higher ground to climb. :-)

My grandma always tells me that to make a great bowl of rice pudding, you've got to use cinnamon sticks. You've got to use cinnamon sticks, and you've got to use vanilla. You can use fresh vanilla bean pods, vanilla powder, or vanilla extract. Just use some form of vanilla. Add some orange zest. This will lift your rice pudding and make all its flavors break into song!

MY GRANDMA'S RICE PUDDING

SERVINGS
4 bowls

NUTRITIONAL DATA PER SERVING
204.4kcals, 10.3g protein, 23.1g carbs, 7g fat, 3.9g fiber

INGREDIENTS

1/2 cup uncooked short-grain rice (I use brown rice)

1/2 cup water

2 cups milk (I use coconut milk, but you can replace it with cow's milk, almond milk, hemp milk, etc.)

1–2 cinnamon sticks

2 tablespoons coconut flour

1/4 cup vanilla brown rice protein powder (vanilla casein protein powder also works a treat here!)

2 tablespoons flaked coconut

Zest of 1 orange

Walnuts or pecans (optional)

Maple syrup (optional)

DIRECTIONS

1. Bring the rice and the water to a boil in a medium-size saucepan.

2. Gradually, add 1 cup of the milk and bring the heat down, so the whole thing simmers.

3. Add the cinnamon stick(s). (The cinnamon stick is just incredible, seriously. It does what cinnamon powder doesn't: it gets in deep.)

4. Simmer for 40 minutes or more, stirring the rice every 10 minutes or so with a wooden spoon, so it doesn't stick to the bottom.

5. Once the rice has cooked, remove the cinnamon stick, place the rice in a big glass bowl, and add the coconut flour, protein powder, flaked coconut, and second cup of milk.

6. Also add the orange zest. If the mixture is too liquid, add a bit more coconut flour or casein protein powder until it gets nice and creamy. If it's too thick, add more milk.

7. Taste it. If you want to kick the whole thing up a notch, consider adding some walnuts or pecans at this stage, too, or a teaspoon or two of maple syrup (sugar-free or regular) for a more maple-y rice pudding.

8. When you're done creating your perfect combo, pour the rice pudding into some ramekins or bowls. Then, when you're (psychologically) ready, grab one of these bowls, take out a spoon, sit down, dig in, and oooooooooh!! Store any leftover pudding in the refrigerator.

THE WORLD'S EASIEST TWO-INGREDIENT PROTEIN PUDDING

This recipe can be made with cooked sweet potato instead of butternut squash. In fact, I bet a lot of people have already done this, because sweet potato or squash with vanilla whey is a wonderful match. Add to that equation a tablespoon or two of peanut or almond butter, and well . . . fwaaaaa! It's fantastic.

SERVINGS
1 bowl

NUTRITIONAL DATA PER SERVING
182.9kcals, 24.2g protein, 18g carbs, 2.6g fat, 2.8g fiber

INGREDIENTS

1/4 cup vanilla whey protein powder

1 cup cooked butternut squash (baked or roasted until soft)

1 tablespoon orange-flavored fish oil or 1 teaspoon grated orange zest (optional, make it 3-ingredient pudding if you use it!

DIRECTIONS

1. Using an immersion blender, blender, or food processor, blend all ingredients together. The orange-flavored fish oil is optional; I like adding it for flavor, but if you don't like the idea of fish oil, you can use the zest.

2. Presto: you've got yourself a protein pudding.

A THREE-INGREDIENT PROTEIN PANNA COTTA

Protein panna cotta: it's kind of like a protein flan but a lot creamier, a lot denser, a lot thicker, a lot more . . . intense. Try it! Try it because you're going to love it—it's ridiculously easy, quick to make, and mmmm. . . . It's one hell of a way to say good-night to your taste buds before you hit the hay. You can top it with fresh berries, with a fresh-fruit coulis, or with some passion fruit for added texture and flavor!

SERVINGS
4 panna cottas

NUTRITIONAL DATA PER SERVING
162kcals, 20g protein, 8g carbs, 5.2g fat

INGREDIENTS
2 cups whole milk

1/4–1/2 cup vanilla casein
        protein powder (depending on how thick you want it)

1 tablespoon plus 1 teaspoon powdered gelatin

DIRECTIONS
1. Heat the milk in a pot to just simmering (you want it to be HOT, but not hot enough to make you scream in agony as you dip a finger in to gauge its temperature).

2. Add the milk to a bowl containing the casein protein powder and gelatin.

3. Whisk everything together as if your life depended on it (because you don't want any chunks in your panna cotta; you want it smooth and creamy, so just keep on whisking).

4. Divide the mixture into four ramekins, bowls, mugs, or whatever, and stick them in the fridge overnight or for several hours.

5. Remove from the fridge and be ready to flip out as you dig into pure deliciousness! Topped with berries = BOOOOM!

I LOVED THIS PANNA COTTA WHEN I MADE IT. FLAVORS RISE AND FALL AS EACH NOTE FOLLOWS THE NEXT WITH A CRESCENDO.

First, you get the smooth creaminess from the coconut, and, as it rises, you get the crunchy staccato from the chia seeds. Then enter the sweet yet tangy sharpness from the black currant sauce followed by a legato of fruity and perfectly balanced port. Ah . . . qu'est-ce qu'on peut dire?

COCONUT & CHIA SEED PROTEIN PANNA COTTA

SERVINGS

2 panna cottas

NUTRITIONAL DATA PER SERVING WITHOUT SAUCE

152kcals, 22g protein, 6.2g carbs, 4.5g fat, 2.4g fiber

NUTRITIONAL DATA PER SERVING WITH SAUCE

189kcals, 22g protein, 16g carbs, 4.5g fat, 2.5g fiber

INGREDIENTS

1 cup coconut milk

1/4 cup coconut whey protein powder

2 tablespoons chia seeds

1 tablespoon plus 1 teaspoon powdered gelatin

1 tablespoon black currant and port sauce (or a
   low-sugar jam or marmalade)

DIRECTIONS

1. Heat the milk in a pot until it's hot but not hot
   enough to burn your finger when you dip it
   into the milk.

2. Pour the milk into a bowl and add to it your
   protein powder, chia seeds, and gelatin.

3. Whisk it together until all powder has
   dissolved.

4. Pour into two silicone flan molds.

5. Place in fridge and leave to set overnight.

6. Turn the mold upside down, top with sauce,
   and BOOM: ready.

LOW-CARB COCONUT PROTEIN BLANCMANGE

Whenever I leaf through cookbooks and cooking magazines, my mind always wanders to "How can I proteinize this?" and I start weaving ingredients in my head until I reach an aha! moment and take to paper. That's kind of what happened here. I saw a recipe for a blueberry blancmange in a food magazine, and I thought, "I've got to try that—with protein!"

SERVINGS

2 blancmanges

NUTRITIONAL DATA PER SERVING

167.5kcals, 27.1g protein, 4.5g carbs, 4.95g fat, 0.2g fiber

INGREDIENTS

1 cup milk

1/2 cup vanilla whey protein powder

1 tablespoon plus 1 teaspoon powdered gelatin

1 tablespoon coconut (or almond) extract

DIRECTIONS

1. First, heat the milk in a pot until it gets hot but not hot enough to burn you if you dip your finger into it.

2. Place the protein powder and gelatin in a glass bowl. Add the hot milk and whisk, whisk, whisk (you want to get rid of ALL lumps with your whisking, so that the final product is nice and smooth). Stir in the extract.

3. Pour the mixture into molds, and place the molds in the fridge for a few hours.

4. Once set, turn them upside down on a plate, press the sides and top of the molds, and BLOP! Here's your blancmange!

CHOCOLATE, COCONUT & BLUEBERRY PROTEIN FLAN

One night, as I was cleaning the kitchen following the war-zoning of the area that accompanied the making of my post-workout meal, I noticed that I have almost an absurd number of boxes of powdered gelatin (I hit up a 10-for-£1 sale a few weeks ago). As soon as I saw all the boxes of powdered gelatin, I thought what I always think when I see powdered gelatin: "Protein flan."

SERVINGS
4 small bowls

NUTRITIONAL DATA PER SERVING
157kcals, 9g protein, 22g carbs, 4g fat, 1g fiber

INGREDIENTS
2 cups coconut or almond chocolate-flavored milk

1/2 cup blueberry whey protein powder (or your flavor of choice)

1 tablespoon plus 1 teaspoon powdered gelatin

DIRECTIONS

1. Heat the milk on the stove until it gets hot-hot—just hot enough to allow you to grab a spoonful of the stuff and taste it without scalding your oral cavity.

2. When the milk is ready, pour it into a bowl and add to it your powder and gelatin.

3. Whisk until all ingredients are well combined.

4. Once you have successfully whisked the whole thing (and no lumps can be found in the milk), pour it into ramekins, bowls, glasses, or mugs, and leave the whole thing in the refrigerator to set overnight.

WHEY TO GO, PROTEIN FLAN!

Anyone could argue that this recipe is somewhat of a repeat of the rest of the flans in this chapter. It kind of is. The only difference here is that, prior to pouring the mixture into individual jelly molds, I let it sit in the bowl for a few minutes, so that the mixture divides a bit as it settles down, to create a kind of layered look.

SERVINGS
4 small bowls
NUTRITIONAL DATA PER SERVING
145kcals, 22.3g protein, 4g carbs, 4g fat, 0.6g fiber

INGREDIENTS
2 cups milk

1/2 cup chocolate whey protein powder

1 1/2 teaspoons powdered gelatin

DIRECTIONS
1. Heat the milk in a pot to just simmering.

2. Pour hot milk into a glass bowl.

3. Add the protein powder and gelatin to the hot milk.

4. Whisk the mixture until it's smooth and all the lumps are gone.

5. Let the mixture sit for a while, and then pour it into jelly molds, bowls, mugs, etc.

6. Leave it in the fridge overnight and . . . barabooom!

7. Enjoy. :-D

BANANA WHEY PROTEIN FLAN

Like the flan before it, this flan uses only three ingredients, and it's unbelieeeevably easy to make. It requires no skill at all and takes no time to make. It's also WAAAAA! So good. Protein flans are one of the best things to make with whey protein powders, I think. Not only are they really easy and quick to make, they're also very filling! So they're a great snack to have. Notice too the ingredients? They're pretty much the same as they are for a protein shake! Only here you're using a spoon instead of a shaker, which makes the whole thing so much more enjoyable, don't you think?

SERVINGS
2 small bowls
NUTRITIONAL DATA PER SERVING
173.7kcals, 27.6g protein, 4.8g carbs, 4.9g fat, 0.5g fiber

INGREDIENTS

2 cups coconut milk (or almond milk,
      hemp milk, or whole milk)
1/2 cup banana whey protein powder
1 tablespoon plus 1 teaspoon powdered gelatin

DIRECTIONS

1. Heat the milk in a pot until it gets hot-hot but not boiling hot. You want to be able to stick your (clean) finger in there without screaming in agony. Think the temperature of coffee or tea.

2. Pour the milk into a bowl and whisk it with the protein powder and gelatin until everything dissolves.

3. Finally, divide the mixture into two bowls (or mugs or glasses), leave it in the fridge overnight until it sets, and BOOOOM!

INDEX

NOTE: Page references in *italics* indicate recipe photographs.

ACKNOWLEDGMENTS

I'd like to thank a few people without whose help and support this book could not have happened. I'd like to first thank my editor, Ann Treistman, for putting Protein Pow on the map, for her support and guidance, and for all the countless hours she spent polishing my drafts to ensure this book shines brightly. Thanks also to Laura Stiers, my copyeditor, for meticulously organizing and editing what have often stood as rambling posts into beautifully structured text. A big thank-you also to Cassie Johnston, this book's designer and, in my eyes, a creative wizard. Cassie is the one who laid out this book, seamlessly integrated my cartoon illustrations, and made this book better than anything I could have dreamed of.

I also want to extend a big thank-you to all the amazing people at W. W. Norton, both in the US and UK, who have made my experience of working on this book really exciting and far less painful than I thought it would be.

Thank you to my friend Stina, for inspiring me to create proteinpow.com and to all my readers and followers at facebook.com/proteinpow who have, from all corners of the world, always supported what I do and encouraged me to follow my passion.

Finally, I'd like to thank the members of my family without whose love and unswerving support Protein Pow and this book would never have come to life.

First I'd like to thank my dad, for being the best dad in the world! He's the force behind my every success and my number one superhero. I'd also like to thank my brother, whose constructive feedback and advice has been invaluable to the creation of this book. A thank-you also goes out to my mom, who, while not present here with us, lives in my heart and inspires me to pursue my dreams with fearlessness, conviction, and always with a smile.

Finally, a colossal thank-you goes out to my husband, Jon, for being the pillar without whom this book (and my entire world with it) would crumble. Thank you for reading everything I write, guinea-pigging so much of my food, believing in me, and generally making my life such an incredible journey! I love you.